The Work Volume II

I Need You, But Where Do We Go From Here?

Benjamin Samuel Brasford

INTELLIGENT PUBLISHING

Columbia, MD
https://intelpub.com

Copyright © 2019 by Benjamin Samuel Brasford.

All rights reserved. Manufactured in the United States of America. No part of this book may be reproduced in any written, electronic, recording, or photocopying form without written permission of the author, except by a reviewer, who may quote brief passages in a review. Published by Intelligent Publishing, P. O. Box 809, Columbia, MD 21044. https://intelpub.com.

THE WORK SERIES

ISBN: 978-1-7329425-4-7 (Paperback)
ISBN: 978-1-7329425-5-4 (E-Book)

Library of Congress Control Number: 2018959821

Portions of this book are works of nonfiction. Certain names and identifying characteristics have been changed.

Book Design by Intelligent Publishing
Editors: Jude A. Daya, William Bernhardt

Printed in the United States of America

First Printing 2019

DEDICATION

This book is dedicated to Gabriel Lightner and Will Barksdale, both who inspired the writing of such from the many conversations that we participated in where intersexual dynamics was the topic. This book is also dedicated to Brandy Hadnot, who never gave up on love.

Contents

DEDICATION	3
ACKNOWLEDGMENTS	7
PREFACE	9
INTRODUCTION	11
1 WORKING TOGETHER OR WORKING APART?	19
Love Based Model Marriage	23
Divorce Becoming the Norm	27
The Workforce	29
2 THE NEW BEGINNING	33
3 YOUR WAY, OUR WAY	37
Cookout	39
4 SAKAYA'S STORY	46
What Love Really Looks Like	54
5 WHERE WE ARE	56
The Male Response to Female Freedom	57
Relationship and Marital Equity	60
Regarding the Social Contract	61
Fertility and Hookup Culture	64
6 WHAT HAPPENS NOW?	68
Marriage Moving Forward	69
The Need For Control	70

Mate Access	72
Out-of-Wedlock Births and No More Shotgun Marriage	72
Social Implications and the Family Moving Forward	74
CONCLUSION	78
SURVEY QUESTIONS	82
ABOUT THE AUTHOR	85
Endnotes	87
Works Cited	88

This page intentionally left blank

ACKNOWLEDGMENTS

Thanks to all that were involved in this project, specifically Volume III of The Work.

This page intentionally left blank

PREFACE

Relationships are vitally important in our everyday life. We need relationships, whether a friendship, acquaintance, sexual, casual, professional, etc. In the current work we focus on marital and non-marital relationships between men and women. We discuss some of the precedents, some of the details of the modern marriage and dating landscape, and where we might be headed. Involved within this work is also story narrative, facts and figures related to the things that are a part of our natural lives whether we are with someone or decide to remain single, and some commentary from the perspective of the author. The story narrative is the continuation of Benjamin and Sakaya's story from chapter seven of "The Work Volume I – The Life of Benjamin Samuel Brasford."

Specific topics such as education, employment, social conditions, economics, finance, government, and how all if not

I NEED YOU, BUT WHERE DO WE GO FROM HERE?

some of these affect the dating market will be fleshed out in quite a bit of detail. As done in "The Work Volume II – Transformation," pertinent words will be defined in the footnotes, there will be an endnotes section as well as works cited.

The current work was inspired by two long-time friends that saw value in the advice that I provided them on intersexual dynamics. After having gone through marriage and many a relationship, I began to read about human behavior and evolutionary psychology. After obtaining a decent understanding of study and observation of men and women, and through trial and error, I began to connect the dots through the observation of behavior instead of focusing primarily on what people said. Analysis of any topic is crucial in the understanding of how to approach things in order to achieve certain levels of success. It is my hope that this information, while disheartening at times, can prove useful to those who find this work to be worthy of being deemed such.

Benjamin Brasford

Maryland
April 25, 2019

INTRODUCTION

INTRODUCTION

As discussed previously in Volumes I and II,[i] I was 20 years old when I entered into a marriage that would last just shy of 16 years. Prior to marriage, I was very naïve and knew very little about women and relationships. My first sexual encounter did not take place until I was 17 years old. The young lady was not originally from my home town, nor did she live in Woods, Atlantis at the time. I do not remember her name nor where she was from. She was a single mother, of a son, and was perhaps two to three years my senior. She was very interested in me and pursued me in a very direct way. She made no mistaking that she wanted to have sex with me. After weeks of talking, kissing, touching, and feeling one another, she would invite me to a hotel room from an establishment of which name I can no longer recollect, purchased the room herself where we spent the night, had sex, and shortly thereafter I would never hear from her again. I did not sleep with some high school sweetheart during my

I NEED YOU, BUT WHERE DO WE GO FROM HERE?

high school years and yet a young lady who was not even from the place that I had finished my childhood and graduated school from, seduced me into having sex with her. I did little to no work at all. She wanted me from the time that she laid eyes on me. I never knew that such things could happen to young men. We went our separate ways and to be honest I did not miss her at all afterwards.

I had had girlfriends from the time that my family moved to Woods, Atlantis. From third grade moving forward, I was never without a young lady who wanted to "go" with me. I had no real clue about how to woo a girl, wasn't very aggressive if at all, and rarely pursued sex with the girls that wanted me. For the most part, the girls that wanted me and those that I "went" with, were attractive. My parents never taught me about relationships and sex in a detailed manner. Since I was from a religious family, the extent of any of those conversations about girls would be that the Bible says to not have sex prior to marriage. Perhaps the religious programming is what gave me such restraint.

Because of the hostile environment of my marriage and the fact that I knew little about maintaining a romantic relationship, my marriage was topsy-turvy for the most part. I had a very difficult time being a husband and father. Having been married at such a young age and never having found myself and what I wanted out of life, this did not help the situation as I am sure that many can imagine. While there were harsh criticisms of Conflict within the first two volumes, to be fair, I was in no shape for taking on the role of husband and father at the time anyway. The churches would only work to keep us married and very often they would

INTRODUCTION

side with Conflict when any problem reared its ugly head throughout the course of our marriage. It was very difficult to withdraw while being in the context of a marriage. The best thing for the both of us was to part ways, despite the fact that Conflict had a child from a previous marriage and that we had had two children together.

I did not learn about the nature of man and woman until after I divorced. I would talk to men and women during the time I was married and following, yet I never felt confident in the advice that I was given. I put much of what I was told into practice and very rarely, if at all, got any real and lasting results. Juggling the re-education of religion, history, and life in general, coming now to the understanding of male/female relationships has been a rough, though rewarding, journey. With middle age approaching, one might ask, "Why go through all of the trouble now?" and, "Since you already had a family even if wasn't successful in the long run, why learn all of this now?" I had come to the conclusion over the years that it is never too late to learn and improve and if I were to be successful in dealing with women, putting in the effort to at least see if I could be was well worth it. My question to the same people that might ask the above questions would be, "If I never had a real shot, why not learn so that I can have a real shot?"

From studying this modern dating and mating scene, I have developed a theory.

"The marriage world dictates the non-marriage world."

I agree with Rollo Tomassi, when he states, *"Men and*

I NEED YOU, BUT WHERE DO WE GO FROM HERE?

women evolved to be complements to the other and in evolutionary terms are far stronger together than apart. Each compensates for the one's innate weaknesses with the other's innate strengths."[1] In today's dating and mating landscape, there is a more adversarial relationship between men and women, generally. Today the woman holds all the cards in reproduction as well as marriage as Akerlof, Yellen and others have observed, due to the fact that the "... *birth of the child the physical choice of the mother, the sexual revolution has made marriage and child support a social choice of the father."*[2] Somehow, though, men are still largely if not entirely the blame for the marriage gap, the birth dearth,[3] and many other if not all ills that causes marriages and relationships to fail. The truth is that that is not the fault of men nor women, at least not alone, but one of many different facets in social change. If anything, one can say that men and women have both assisted in the changes, whether willingly or unwillingly.

While there are a goodly number of bachelors and spinsters by choice living in the U.S., as well as other Western countries, the end goal for many non-marital relationships is to someday be married. Cohabitating relationships, general-

---

1 (Tomassi, The Myth of the Alpha Female)
2 (George A. Akerlof)
3 Birth dearth is a neologism referring to falling fertility rates. In the late 1980s, the term was used in the context of American and European society. The use of the term has since been expanded to include many other industrialized nations. It is often cited as a response to overpopulation, but is not incompatible with it. The term was coined by Ben Wattenberg in his 1987 book by that same name. (Wikipedia, Birth dearth)

INTRODUCTION

ly, do not desire to marry.[4] Cohabitating couples tend to be far more happier than marriages and place far less expectations upon one another. If the marriage market is bad, that sets the tone for the non-marriage market. As marriage has declined, cohabitation has been on the rise.[5] This rise in cohabitation is not just an American phenomenon. It is a Western one. There are many bachelors and spinsters who have fell into those categories by default, while blame is being thrown on both sides for such circumstances. To be honest, there are some people who just don't want to be married and they intend to enjoy relationships whether casual or otherwise in a hedonistic[6] way for the rest of their lives without any desire to have children. This is not the overwhelming majority, though, some may believe otherwise.

Government policy has affected many aspects of the way the opposite sexes approach one another. Marriage is a legal union. Cohabitation is not a legal union, per se, due to laws that govern people differently that haven't been recognized by the state. Only after so much time are cohabitating partners recognized on a more legal footing, being termed either common law marriages[7] or domestic partnerships[8] depend-

---

4   ("The Retreat From Marriage': Summary of a Discussion 102), (Smith 11), (Kathryn Edin, 3. How Does the Dream Die? 90)
5   (Vitali and Berrington)
6   Hedonistic - Engaged in the pursuit of pleasure; sensually self-indulgent. (Oxford University Press, hedonistic, adj. 1)
7   Common Law – 2. [as modifier] Denoting a partner in a marriage recognized in some jurisdictions (excluding the UK) as valid by common law, though not brought about by a civil or ecclesiastical ceremony. 2.1. Denoting a partner in a relationship in which a man and woman cohabit for a period long enough to suggest stability. (Oxford University Press, common law, n.2)
8   Domestic Partner – 2. : either one of an unmarried heterosex-

I NEED YOU, BUT WHERE DO WE GO FROM HERE?

ing upon the legal jurisdictional state. The laws are more in favor of the woman. This is a fact that some women that I have come across either are unaware of or are in outright denial of. In fact, women initiate the vast majority of the divorces.[9] As stated above from Rollo Tomassi, the sexes having evolved to be complementary, there are many stating that the ideal is now to have more egalitarian relationships. This may sound nice in theory, yet in practice, it rarely if at all fares well in the real world. That's the thing with theory, *"A supposition or a system of ideas intended to explain something, especially one based on general principles independent of the thing to be explained."*[10] It is great when it is based on general principles independent of the thing to be explained. The problem with the egalitarian model, is that it is not based on general principles independent of the thing or relationship between a man and a woman to be explained. Some have posited that it is based on a utopian, Marxist, Platonist, Leftist, etc. ideology or set of ideologies that are diametrically opposed to the evolved psychological and biological ways that men and women have worked for thousands of years.[11] Book after book, article after article, etc., have been published and reported trying to sell this egalitarian model and it has yet to take hold and yield a real-world conclusion. This egalitarian model has been well observed to be a deferring to the feminine or female ways of thought and doing things. I agree wholeheartedly with Rollo Tomassi's assessment,

---

ual or homosexual cohabiting couple especially when considered as to eligibility for spousal benefits. (Merriam Webster Dictionary)

9 (American Sociological Association)
10 (Oxford University Press, theory, n.1.)
11 (Tomassi, BLUE PILL CONDITIONING AND EQUALISM)

INTRODUCTION

"Adopting a mindset that accepts complementarity between the sexes and between individuals, one that celebrates and utilizes innate strengths and talents, yet also embraces the weaknesses and compensates for them is a far healthier one that presuming baseline equivalency. Understanding the efficacy of applying strengths to weaknesses cooperatively while acknowledging we all aren't the same damn dog will be a key to dissolving the fantasy of egalitarian equalism and create a more balanced and healthier relations between the sexes. Embracing the fact that condition, environment, reality and the challenges they pose defines our usefulness is far better than to assume any single individual could ever be a self-contained, self-sufficient island unto themselves – that is what equalism would have us believe."[12]

The egalitarian equalist model is a very dangerous and erroneous mindset that has exacerbated many a relationship and many a marriage.

This third volume will attempt to un-hash the above theory in detail by covering some of what has happened, some of where we are, and perhaps where we might be going moving forward. The details involve what I believe are specific societal changes. With the impact of the societal changes of the legal environment, the shift from the old model to the new model of love-based marriages, the workforce changes of more women working, more men leaving the workforce and the wage gap, the college education factor, cohabitation, and out-of-wedlock births, we are able to come to a more complete understanding of how we have arrived at where we are in regards to the marriage and the non-marriage scene.

---

12   (Tomassi, THE LIE OF EQUALITY)

I NEED YOU, BUT WHERE DO WE GO FROM HERE?

There will be no solutions, though some suggestions will be given from time to time. I take the position that solutions are up to the individual person to find and not necessarily using someone else's script. So, let us begin our exploration into our modern marriage and non-marriage scene.

1 WORKING TOGETHER OR WORKING APART?

"COMMUNITIES ARE MADE OF FAMILIES. HOW STRONG OR WEAK THOSE FAMILIES ARE WILL DETERMINE THE STRENGTH OR WEAKNESS OF THOSE COMMUNITIES." - BENJAMIN SAMUEL BRASFORD

The landscape for relationships today is not as it was in the past. Courting is nothing new, but the way that we court today has changed over the years. One of the few areas that can make or break a relationship, whether a long-term relationship or a marriage, is finance.[13] When dealing with finance many factors come into play and the changes over time matter much more than many may realize. Whether one or the both of you have jobs or operate your own business(es), factors historical as well as future projected should be carefully considered if you in-

---

13   Finance - 1.2 finances The monetary resources and affairs of a state, organization, or person. (Oxford University Press, finance, n.1)

I NEED YOU, BUT WHERE DO WE GO FROM HERE?

tend for your relationship to work for the long haul. The United States has undergone several transitions within the distant and in recent years. This country will continue to go through changes which is why a couple must keep the importance of their financial health in mind. Communities are made of families. How strong or weak those families are will determine the strength or weakness of those communities.

Why is finance or capital so important, one might ask? It is what drives business and economics. As observed by Musselman and Hughes, *"...business and economics are mutually complementary."*[14] Business, a person's regular occupation, profession, or trade,[15] and economics, the branch of knowledge concerned with the production, consumption, and transfer of wealth,[16] is how we are able to care for and further our families. How effective we are at these is very important. Finance is not everything. A relationship needs a combination of love, affection, attention, time, communication, understanding, emotional support, intimacy, sex, collaboration, mutuality, etc.[17] But we must pay bills, eat, have a roof over our heads, be able to purchase gifts for one another, and do things together whether at home or in public.

Marriage needs financing, yes, but finance is just one part of what is needed in order for a marriage to work. Marriage may have at one time been an instrument,[18] but over time it

---

14   (Vernon A. Musselman 3)
15   (Oxford Univeristy Press, Definition of business in English:)
16   (Oxford Univeristy Press, Definition of economics in English:)
17   (Goldsmith)
18   "… a social organization that is fulfilling effectively the purpose for which it arose." (Quigley 101-102)

1 WORKING TOGETHER OR WORKING APART?

became an institution, as Stephanie Coontz observes, *"... marriage has been, in one form or another, a universal social institution throughout recorded history."*[19] Our modern scene for marriage has changed tremendously from the pre-1950s. In previous times, marriage was much more about finances and politics.[20] They were about the extended family connections for the purpose of resources and concerning the children to secure the future. There were certain economic benefits to marriage as well as benefits of the social safety net and even access to unemployment insurance. Marriage was also about power and social status. It was class-based and used as a tool to keeping out those that were not part of a certain grouping or family clique. Married people were seen as responsible, reliable, and were considered adults. Marriage was desired by most because there was a certain level of respect that those who were married automatically received, with it being the institution that it was. Even today, there are many who see married people at a higher level than those who are single. Some are even shamed by not having been married by a certain age, and that is not according to a particular gender.

We have come to understand marriage today to be based upon love. Love is a beautiful thing. We fall in love all the time. It is not a logical thing. One will make some of the most irrational decisions when one is in love with someone. The funny thing about it is, when you're in love, you don't care about being rational anyway. All you care about is talking with the person, being near them, touching them and you're thinking about them all throughout the day. You

---

19 (Coontz, The Many Meanings of Marriage 24)
20 (Coontz, Soap Operas of the Ancient World)

I NEED YOU, BUT WHERE DO WE GO FROM HERE?

cannot wait to be with them again. You make plans in your mind and even contemplate what happened before as well as ponder on what might happen next. This is a luxury today for in the past, this was not so.

Some have recognized, though, that marriage being based upon love is unstable. The reason why it is unstable is because, just as one can fall in love, one can fall out of love just as easily. When love-based marriage arrived on the scene, so did the desire to divorce as well. It seems that with every good thing comes a nemesis.[21] It is similar to the gift of freedom: the more freedom bestowed, the greater the possibility of losing it becomes available. Marriage had many restraints in the past. Now there is much more freedom available in marriages and relationships in general. The only real restraints today seem to be how we allow the dictates of the broader society to affect us.

In my first marriage, having married so young, I had no clue as to what it meant to be a husband. I watched my father growing up but he was very hands off as a husband and father. Providing for the family through his job was all he seemed to understand was important. I lacked a model within his particular demonstration over the years. With my marriage being arranged, and arranged by church leaders, I just followed as best I could, depending upon how I felt at the time, what I was told. Imagine being married to someone that you do not know, trying to emulate something to them with no genuine feelings towards them. When we say we love someone, we love something about them. It's some-

---

21   Nemesis - The inescapable agent of someone's or something's downfall. (Oxford University Press, nemesis, n.1)

1 WORKING TOGETHER OR WORKING APART?

thing or there are some things that we love about them. It's the same thing when we say that we don't like or cannot stand someone. We cannot stand something about them. In my marriage it was as if everything was an act. That is very difficult to do on a daily basis. Not only are you acting, but you are then producing children with this person that you are acting with because you have no past to establish any level of familiarity with. You love the children but you are acting with who you are having a child with. Try and wrap your mind around that one.

Over time, we did grow to have some genuine feelings for each other. The problem is that our beginning stages was surrounded by pain, confusion, manipulation, deception, and it generally moved too fast. Where confusion abounds, evil resides. My wife at the time, Conflict, conceived our first child within the first month of marriage! Here I was twenty years old, only having been away from home two years, about to reach the legal age to drink, in a place where I knew no one to include my wife, I had no plan, and received guidance from two people who over time hated me as if the entire thing was my fault.

Love Based Model Marriage

An entire new set of values were established to govern love and marriage about two centuries ago. Stephanie Coontz observes,

> *"In this Western model, people expect marriage to satisfy more of their psychological and social needs than ever before. Marriage is supposed to be free of the coercion, violence, and gender inequalities that were tolerated in the*

I NEED YOU, BUT WHERE DO WE GO FROM HERE?

past. Individuals want marriage to meet most of their needs for intimacy and affection and all their needs for sex."[22]

This is generally what I had heard for the greater part of my life. I did not know, but did find out, that marriage at one time was arranged by the parents of the man and the woman. That is unheard of in our modern times. We have gotten so used to being free, as free as we can be or believe to be, that there are areas that many of us refuse to forgo by allowing others to tell us what we should and should not do. We take for granted that our freedom came with a cost, and alongside that cost is the ever-nagging possibility of it being sacrificed upon the altar of poor choices. While marriage became more about love than the old model, marriage was still yet on the verge of decline by the 1950s and 1960s.[23] There was a significant decline by the 1970s in marriage. Things had gone from bad to worse by the 1990s.[24] Marriages remaining intact even for the sake of children was not enough; as Herbert L. Smith observes, there came,

"... a declining belief that marriages should remain intact "for the sake of the children" (London 1989, p. 2), and it may be the case that the positive effect of children on marital stability is declining."[25]

---

22 (Coontz, Chapter 1: The Radical Idea of Marrying for Love 23)
23 (Coontz, Introduction 8)
24 (Rosin 94-95)
25 (Smith 20) "Republished with permission of University Press of America, Inc., from The Retreat from Marriage: Causes and Consequences, Bryce J. Christensen, 1999; permission conveyed through Copyright Clearance Center, Inc."

1 WORKING TOGETHER OR WORKING APART?

The old model of marriage, though it was at times arranged, as well as dictated by the extended families, was relatively short lived. Industrialization changed the dynamics of work and home.[26] As time marched on, people wanted to do marriage differently. There were enormous social and economic changes that took place around the 1950s to the 1970s that would also affect the 1980s and the 1990s.[27] As women began to enter into the workforce, this alone had its own affects on how family would be conducted in the future. Women were now able to economically fend for themselves without the need of a man. This would give women more negotiating power in order to command the mate that they wanted to be with instead of settling or by circumstance remaining with the man that they otherwise would not be with. This was all due to the movements of Equal Rights[28] and Feminism.[29] Feminism became a response to the demographic changes that were evident. Smith explains,

"The extreme...goal of the feminist movement, ...the rejection of all division of labor based on sex, ...is understandable, because it extrapolates to its end the actual diminution

---

26   (Smith 25)
27   See Stephanie Coontz' "Marriage, a History: How Love Conquered Marriage" Chapter 15: Winds of Change:
Marriage in the 1960s and 1970s
28   Proposed as Equal Rights Amendment (ERA) was introduced by Alice Paul, suffragist leader, in 1923, after the 19th Amendment was ratified in 1920. It is still currently undergoing ratification by the states, as passed on from Congress.
29   A result of various political, ideological, and social movements for the purposes of common goals between the sexes. Became prominent during the French and American revolutions in the late 1700s, and later in Britain in the late 1800s. Was presented as a second wave in the 1960s, and as a third wave in the late 1980s and 1990s.

I NEED YOU, BUT WHERE DO WE GO FROM HERE?

of marriage and childbearing in women's lives...(Davis and van den Oever 1982, pp. 508-509)."[30]

With some of the ways that marriage was seen as it began to change around the 1970s to 1990s, one way was a hedonistic version, where people focused on their own individual needs according to the values of society at that time.[31] People were more interested in modeling what others were doing. Men also seemed to no longer care about their traditional roles as long as they could get what they wanted out of the women who desired to deal with them.[32]

In the days of my first marriage, not only did Conflict and I do what we could to emulate what we thought other married couples were doing, but our married peers were doing the same. We are social creatures and desire to do what others do. It has to do with acceptance. Carroll Quigley observes that one of the six basic human needs is group security. We have a basic need for acceptance and will thereby do what we can at times in order to be accepted by those whose opinions we value. More than any others, those that are close to us, personally, we desire to be accepted by them. We will often even act as they do through dress, extracurricular activities, and even social grouping by way of church, sports, cookouts, and even vacationing together. I often heard people say, and even I have said at times, that they do not care about what other people think. That may be true

---

30 (Smith 26) "Republished with permission of University Press of America, Inc., from The Retreat from Marriage: Causes and Consequences, Bryce J. Christensen, 1999; permission conveyed through Copyright Clearance Center, Inc."
31 (Glenn 34)
32 (Smith 25-26)

1 WORKING TOGETHER OR WORKING APART?

to some degree but it is not entirely accurate. We all care about what other people think, especially depending upon who that person is in relation to what we may need or desire. This shows just how important our cultural environment really is. Culture is very important and it changes over time. What is normal or is the norm now will not be normal or the norm over time. Since the physical world, observable reality, is irrational as Quigley rightly asserted, we are unable to grasp much of how it operates. Culture is our insulation between the natural environment and ourselves, though it penetrates us as well as our natural environment. The very purpose of culture and its parts is people's effort to satisfy their own needs, individually and collectively.[33]

Divorce Becoming the Norm

"The U.S. has almost definitely reached the point where over half of all marriages contracted annually will end in divorce." – Herbert L. Smith[34]

As stated earlier, with marriage changing to a love-based model, the freedom of choice in marriage became the dominant way of conducting marriage, based upon fulfilling one's needs and desires within this context. Along with that freedom also came the choice of alleviating oneself from being with someone as well. Divorce, too, has become the norm in modern society, as a result. Specifically speaking, with

---

33 (Quigley 101)
34 (Smith 21) "Republished with permission of University Press of America, Inc., from The Retreat from Marriage: Causes and Consequences, Bryce J. Christensen, 1999; permission conveyed through Copyright Clearance Center, Inc. ", (Kathryn Edin, 4. What Marriage Means 134-135)

I NEED YOU, BUT WHERE DO WE GO FROM HERE?

social, economic, and cultural change also comes changes within the legal environment. Sometimes the legal changes dictate culture and society, and at other times the culture and the society dictate legal changes. One such change for the new model of marriage was no-fault divorce.[35] The name no-fault is exactly what it implies, meaning no fault or reason for breaking the parameters of the marriage bond. It is now easy to get married, and it is easy to get divorced. It is also cheap to get married, but generally not cheap to get divorced. The fact that it is not cheap to get divorced has by default caused much fear in many in making a decision to get married in the first place.

Divorce actually began much earlier than I had come to realize. It apparently began as early as the 1950s. That is well before the no-fault divorce rates that took place in the 1970s.[36] As hearkened to above, economics played a major factor within the changes that took place in regard to marriage. Again, as women entered the workforce, they were given more freedom of choice and with this freedom, marriages that they found unfulfilling, they began to leave behind.[37] With opportunity comes desire, and with desire comes seeking, and with seeking goes the person out of your

---

35 No fault divorce is the dissolution of a marriage which does not require evidence of wrongdoing by the man or woman. It only requires that the man or woman petitions the court to grant them the right to be freed, legally, from the marriage without having to prove a marital breach of the contract. California was the first state, passed by then Governor Ronald Reagan, to adopt no fault divorce, which provided an avenue for the others states to adopt this model as well.

36 (Coontz, Chapter 15: Winds of Change: Marriage in the 1960s and 1970s 252)

37 (Rosin 93)

1 WORKING TOGETHER OR WORKING APART?

life if you are not providing what they are looking for. It was women who now had a say in what they wanted. It was women who began to chart their own courses. Women who not only took on more jobs, but also more education.

The Workforce

It would seem that there are many degrees to the status of women in our modern era. While there are some women who are not doing well in regard to education nor economics, some women are faring quite well. Many women are making more than their own husbands. Whether women are married, single with no children, or are single mothers, these women undoubtedly do not need men to finance them in any way. The single without children and single mothers who might have education or not, and who are not doing well financially may not be the norm as many have thought. From the Civil Rights Act and the Equal Pay Act, more and more women have come into the labor force. Women even outnumber men when it comes to college enrollment.[38]

Liza Mundy observes that we are entering a time where women will be the majority breadwinners in the home. The percentage of women who were breadwinners in 1970 was very low. Fast forward to forty years later and, *"Almost 40 percent of U.S. working wives now outearn their husbands, a percentage that has risen steeply in this country and many others, as more women have entered the workforce and remained committed to it."*[39]

Women dominate more than half of the managerial and

---

38   (Carnevale, Smith and Gulish 9)
39   (Mundy 6)

I NEED YOU, BUT WHERE DO WE GO FROM HERE?

professional jobs as well as almost all of the ten of the expected growth job categories. In regard to earnings, *"In most American cities, single childless women between 22 and 30 make more, in terms of median income, than their male peers, a direct result of the fact that women are now better-educated than men."*[40]

Some argue that women are still choosing traditional majors within college and are still taking on more traditional jobs. Women seem to focus on majors within the fields of healthcare, business, psychology, social sciences, history, and education.[41] There is also the discussion of the wage gap which has had and still has proponents for and opponents against. The gap in earnings between men and women depend on many factors and cannot be based on simple answers. It is largely due to college major and career choices. The choices once those careers are chosen and worked within also come into play.[42,43]

With more and more women becoming more employable and more educated, and with men in general not doing as well as a group, this places the women who desire marriage at a disadvantage if they desire marriage or relationships via assortative mating.[44] According to a report by the Brookings

---

40   (Mundy 9)
41   (Carnevale, Smith and Gulish 20)
42   (Carnevale, Smith and Gulish 20)
43   (Mundy, Part One: The Overtaking 56)
44   "Assortative mating, in human genetics, a form of nonrandom mating in which pair bonds are established on the basis of phenotype (observable characteristics). For example, a person may choose a mate according to religious, cultural, or ethnic preferences, professional interests, or physical traits.

1 WORKING TOGETHER OR WORKING APART?

Institution, *"There is a growing trend in the United States towards assortative mating—a clunky phrase that refers to people's tendency to choose spouses with similar educational attainment. Rising numbers of college-educated women play a key role in this change. It is much easier for college graduates to find and marry each other when there are more equal numbers of each gender within an educational bracket."*[45] The issue is, as Nicholas Eberstadt and others have observed, American men have been leaving the labor force since the post-World War II era.[46] As women have improved across the board, men as a group have not. Mr. Eberstadt observes,

"No matter their race or educational status, married men raising a family work more, and never-married men without children or children in their home work less. No matter their ethnicity or race, prime-age men who come to this country work more than those here by birth. Neither a wedding ring nor a green card confers innate advantage in the competition for jobs. Rather, marriage and migration decisions point to motivations, aspirations, priorities, values, and other intangibles that do so much to explain real-world human achievements."[47]

Positive assortative mating, or homogamy, exists when people choose to mate with persons similar to themselves (e.g., when a tall person mates with a tall person); this type of selection is very common. Negative assortative mating is the opposite case, when people avoid mating with persons similar to themselves. (T. E. Britannica)

45   (Reeves and Rodrigue)
46   (Eberstadt, Chapter 1: The Collapse of Work in the Second Gilded Age 17), (Kathryn Edin, 4. What Marriage Means 135)
47   (Eberstadt, Chapter 5: Who Is He? A Statistical Portrait of the

I NEED YOU, BUT WHERE DO WE GO FROM HERE?

Marriage provides an avenue to have different motivations. Some have stated that married men, while they do work more hours and generally do better, are more responsible.[48] This makes sense when you consider that when a person is responsible for others besides themselves, those motivations will cause them to work harder by default. Motivation, premise, or proposition, is key in understanding behavior when we are trying to get to the why behind a person. Drive and ambition and several other key words communicate the modus operandi of any individual. It has to do with intentions that can only be known when a person speaks what they are, or when others who are keen enough to pick up on nuances of the speech or the behavior of the individual. So, men as well as women are driven from motivations that are unique to their individual selves and philosophies. So with men not working as much, being less educated, being less motivated, women who are looking for men to be at their levels, at least some of them, are at certain disadvantages.[ii] Others have rightly observed that finances are not the only breakdown to a relationship.[49] It is true, though, that money and education are important when it comes to the consideration of marriage as opposed to cohabitation.[50] It is these aspects of our reality, which are multi-faceted and untenable to be placed upon one explanation or one individual cause, that are in dire need for exploration.

Un-Working American Man 70)
48 (Eberstadt, Chapter 5: Who Is He? A Statistical Portrait of the Un-Working American Man 70)
49 (Kathryn Edin 75)
50 (Whelan)

2 THE NEW BEGINNING

A gentle caress of her hand as he gazes into her eyes at the dawn of the sunrise. The coffee has finished brewing and the aroma permeates the entire house. She smiles at him while grinning from ear to ear just before he picks her up and places her upon the countertop about two feet from the sink. They kiss gently to begin with and all of a sudden as if in unison they both become passionate. He begins to pull off her night gown when - "Mommy, I'm hungry," says the little girl. The little girl, named Sakoya, begins to pull Benjamin's pajama pants leg as if she was the boss of the home. Benjamin and Sakaya look at one another as if they both understood that the ensuing encounter would commence later.

Sakoya, now three years old, just loved her mommy and desired to be just like her. That did not mean that she wasn't

I NEED YOU, BUT WHERE DO WE GO FROM HERE?

still a daddy's little girl. She knew how to get what she wanted out of him even at the tender age of three.

"Hey baby, did you sleep good?" Benjamin asks Sakoya. "Yes daddy," she replies while smiling and spinning into a dance.

After getting dressed, Benjamin and Sakaya kiss as if it was the first time that they laid eyes on one another. As if they had fallen in love for the first time. They hug as if they were not going to see each other again for a while. Benjamin kisses Sakoya on the cheek and gives her a big hug before Sakaya straps her in the car seat of the Range Rover to head off to private school and then the office. Benjamin gets into his 535i, to head to the office. The suburbs outside of Metropola, Peaceful Hills, is where not only Benjamin and his family lives, but also where the Stewarts, Jonathan and Sarah, who were married with two children, also live. They often got together on the weekends for leisure. Jonathan and Benjamin attended college together. Benjamin managed to obtain an MBA and a PMI certification which landed him the position of department head of Business Development and Construction Administration at the architectural firm that Jonathan, an architect, started. The logging business was now long left behind.

Benjamin and Sakaya were now married and very happy. Their relationship got even better post marriage, so much so that they began to be a model for other relationships. Over the years, Benjamin had learned about how men and women interact through the study of evolutionary psychology.[51] He

---

51   (Kenrick)

2 THE NEW BEGINNING

concluded that when men and women work within complementarity, both parties benefit and the relationship thrives. Benjamin had accepted the failures of his first marriage and continued to pour himself into studies and practice. This time, he was able to choose his woman. Sakaya responded to his request and returned his affection. Over time the chemistry between them was electric. In public, they rarely kept their hands off one another. When in restaurants, they sat next to each other, touching, gazing often into one another's eyes, and even kissing occasionally. No matter how many conversations they had, neither of them ever got bored with the other. There were those who attacked their relationship. Some did not believe that such a thing could be genuine. Benjamin developed the mindset to protect his marriage with Sakaya. He petitioned to her to not entertain anyone nor anything that would sow the seeds of destruction of their union. He accepted that many would not understand. He would, however, allow no one to hinder the growing love and affection that his wife and he had for one another.

Sakaya was in the marketing business. She provided marketing services to mid-sized and small businesses involved in manufacturing products to include toiletries, stationary, indie book publishing, indie film making, indie music, and graphic design. She had written a book about her life, which included her love experiences with Benjamin. It was she who first decided that Benjamin and her should tell other people about their relationship. Benjamin was reluctant at first, wanting to keep their love a secret. Sakaya wanted very much for the world to know about what she had with him, though, she was very careful to not give too much detail. She was like a little girl with him, in the sense that when-

I NEED YOU, BUT WHERE DO WE GO FROM HERE?

ever he talked and she was around, her attention was fixed upon him. In pictures, her gaze in the majority of the photos were fixed on him. She adored him. It was as if she was the opposite of Conflict, Benjamin's first wife. But as much as she was into him, Benjamin was just as much into her. Their love was magnetic. When they were with others, even family, these other people would either be happy for them, or hate that they had such a wonderful relationship. So, Sakaya insisted on telling the world about a portion of what she and Benjamin were experiencing. Perhaps such a love is rare. Some would say that it is just a story and can never exist. In a world full of grey, there is a little bit of everything. Love it or hate it, Sakaya's book did really well. And the love that she and Benjamin have, still exists and is stronger than when it first began.

3 YOUR WAY, OUR WAY

"What's up, man?" says D to Benjamin.

"I'm good man, what's been up with you?"

"Nothing much man. I see you and Sakaya were like the perfect match man. That's what's up," D replies.

"Yeah man, you never know what might happen. Had I not come to the business summit, I would not have received your advice not only on business, but I also probably would have never met Sakaya," says Benjamin.

"Well, stuff happens when it's supposed to man. I am truly happy for the both of you," D replies.

D or Darryn, now officially a mentor of Benjamin, was a commercial developer involved in quite a few projects in

I NEED YOU, BUT WHERE DO WE GO FROM HERE?

downtown Metropola, as well as other cities and even states. He also played the stock market very well. He had an on-going mentoring relationship with one of the richest men of not only Metropola, but in the greater regional and even international arena. After all, Darryn's mentor was not only a banker, but also involved directly and indirectly into farming, oil, and mining. So, Darryn was privileged to have met Mr. Preston Stockworth. One of the wealthiest and most private men alive. Private in the sense of his public life and private life were far more different than most were aware of.

Darryn, still not married and with no intentions on becoming married, saw a regular pool of women on a fairly regular basis. He was not the type to be tied down to one woman. Unfortunately, he was at one time, the type to deal with not only other men's girlfriends, but even other men's wives. One thing Darryn was good at was entertaining women and almost 100% successful in getting them to go home with him.

He had everything that a woman could want aesthetically. He had the cars, four of them. He had the homes, a condominium downtown, a house in the suburbs, and three other homes for rent. He dressed right, suits, upscale casual, and expensive shoes. He was slim, muscular, and 6'-4" in height. He was a rich man who had gotten an early start in his money acquisition and management. Well connected, his brother and him, Jarrod, an inch taller and involved in the trafficking of drugs as well as other methods of the dark side, had at one time been involved in illicit activities. Darryn, had over time, decided to break away from the criminal side and go legit.

3 YOUR WAY, OUR WAY
Cookout

It was a hot summer day in Darryn's backyard, and the grill was full of hamburgers, chicken leg quarters, corn on the cob, and red snapper. In the kitchen, Shanice, Darryn's sister, preparing cabbage, kale, and sweet potatoes, says to her husband James,

"Go outside and tell Darryn that everything is ready."

James says, "Okay, baby."

James goes out immediately to tell Darryn that the food in the kitchen is ready. Darryn replies, "Cool man."

Jarrod, while sitting at the table in the dining area, shakes his head after thinking hard about how Shanice talked to and often talks to James. Jarrod thought even deeper about how James just takes it and never says anything back to Shanice. James often goes along to get along with his wife. Over the years, Shanice had lost much respect for him. She began to treat him as a child. What he failed to realize was that you will be treated based upon what you allow.

Jarrod was rough around the edges and quick to anger. He was not the type to allow you to just do or say anything to him. He was always ready for a fight. Well suited for the business of the streets, he worked his way up to living within the suburbs, Right Way, where he now had others doing the dirty work for him. So, Jarrod was able to give the appearance that he was a normal working man, well dressed, well groomed, and an auto-didactic in education where he could

I NEED YOU, BUT WHERE DO WE GO FROM HERE?

hold conversations with the best of them. Never having gone to college, he still out-earned the majority of those within his neighborhood.

Jarrod stays out of business that is not his own. Today, he decided to stick his nose in the business of his sister and her husband.

"James, bruh, let me holler at you for a minute," says Jarrod while summoning him to go outside as he was headed to the grill near Darryn. "Dude, you have got to grab a shovel, head out in your backyard and dig up some backbone. You have allowed this disrespect from my sister towards you to go on too long. At some point, she is either going to leave you, or she is going to start cheating on you. Bruh, that's my sister, and I am telling you that you need to get into her shit to let her know that you are no longer going to tolerate that bullshit," says Jarrod.

"Man, I'm not built like you and Darryn, man. I don't want her to leave me, man. I love her. She's so beautiful and smart. I don't even know why she chose me. I will never get another woman like her," exclaims James.

"What the fuck are you talking about? She is beautiful, but don't let that stop you from being a fucking man. Beautiful, mediocre, or ugly, a woman doesn't admire a man that she can control. She can get away with what she says and does. That's not how this shit works. Even if you make less than her, you can still be a man that has backbone as my brother says. Fuck that, man. You are so afraid of losing her that you are going to end up losing her anyway. Even if you don't lose

3 YOUR WAY, OUR WAY

her, she will continue to treat you like a child and eventually stop fucking you. Snap out of it, man," says Darryn.

James now looked at Darryn puzzled. Darryn and Jarrod were very good with women. They were the type of men that women wanted. They were the type of men that other men wanted to be. Knowing that Jarrod was a street guy, James still looked up to him. It was not a secret to the family that Jarrod not only had a past, but it was a secret to some that he was still very much involved in illicit activity. Even his sister, Shanice, had been steeped into that past. She wanted James because he was safe. She knew that James would take care of her and never leave her. They had three children, two daughters, 5 and 7, and one son who was the oldest at 15. So, Shanice used this knowledge as leverage. The truth, too, was that Shanice had cheated on James several times, and had even been involved in successful side relationships. Long hours at work gave her opportunity to engage in encounters with men on the job. Even business trips were taken at times as cover for actual extra-marital relationships and affairs.

James, looking at Darryn sharply, "Man, she is your sister. Do you really think she's that way, man? I just can't believe it. Why would she leave me when I have never hit her, cheated on her, talk down to her, nor ignored her?"

"Man, you don't understand women at all. You really think that all of that is going to save you? Everything you just said doesn't imply a man as a lover at all. It all implies a man being a friend and one who doesn't want to rock the boat. Women need emotion, good or bad, especially if she's going to see you as a sexual man. Sex needs tension of some

I NEED YOU, BUT WHERE DO WE GO FROM HERE?

sort. You should either flirt, or not always agree with her. You need to generate emotion. Being her friend is okay at times but don't agree as a yes-man. I'm not talking about being mean. I'm talking about having the mindset of a man. Also, having something to do that doesn't keep you around her all of the time. Having a purpose. A plan. And making sure you are executing that plan. I know you love her and love being around her, but believe it or not, a woman doesn't want to see her man not doing anything with his time. When you two come back together, you need to have shown that you were busy. Your life and actions should imply that," says Darryn.

The doorbell rings, and Shanice opens the door to Benjamin, Sakaya, and Sakoya.

"Hey y'all," says Shanice.

"Hey," say Benjamin and Sakaya.

After saying hi and waving to Shanice, Sakoya runs over to play with Deidra and Shantell. John, the eldest son of James and Shanice, is in one of Darryn's guestrooms occupied with Red Dead Redemption 2 on the PlayStation 4. Sakaya sits down at the dining room table with Shanice and Sandra. Sandra is a friend of Shanice's from the law firm, Simms and Bradley Law, located on the 4200 block of 7th Street, downtown. She was just as successful at law as Shanice. Single, no children, and having had a numerous amount of bad relationships and flings, she was beginning to worry if she would ever be married. She did not possess the best of attitudes and was often out of touch with reality. Shanice began spending a good amount of time with her due to often noticing her

3 YOUR WAY, OUR WAY

moodiness and noticing how she couldn't seem to keep a guy as a boyfriend for longer than six months.

"So, how you been Sandra? Meet anyone new lately?" asks Shanice.

"Girl, I am tired of these sorry-assed men out here. I can't seem to keep anyone longer than six months. Hell, the last guy and I didn't even last three months. It's like it is really good and interesting for a while, and then it all falls off of a cliff! They are all fake. They present themselves like they have their shit together, and then it becomes clear that they are all faking. I don't get it!" Sandra replies.

"Sandra, what do you want? I thought that you were cool with seeing who you chose to see when you choose to see them," says Shanice.

"I want to be married. I'm tired of the casual thing. I want a family. I feel like time is running out. I didn't want all of that when I was younger. But I see you and Sakaya married with children, and I'm still single!" says Sandra.

"Marriage is okay. I mean James is nice and we never argue. He pretty much does what I say. We both have odd work schedules. We have routines for chores and picking up the kids. But then again, John is old enough now to help out with watching the girls. So, we're good," says Shanice.

"Shanice. Everything that you just said is pertaining to functioning of the duties of a marriage. It's okay, I guess. But do you ever spend time together outside of that? Do you

I NEED YOU, BUT WHERE DO WE GO FROM HERE?

both do things together? Also, how often do you both express your love for one another?" asks Sakaya.

"Girl. Look. Everybody is not like y'all. I know that y'all are all in love and shit. Can't keep your hands off of one another. Don't like being apart. That's all good. And I have to admit, I thought that shit wasn't going to last between you two. But here we are four years down the road and it seems like it may be even stronger. Congratulations to you both. Everybody ain't got that shit, Ky," says Shanice.

"Wow. That's what y'all have? I want that too. Every guy I get with, they seem to only care about sex and little to no affection, at least until we start having sex regularly," says Sandra.

"Well, I have heard that some things are rare. Whatever the case, I'm not letting it go. I love B and as long as I can experience this with him, that's exactly what the hell I'm going to do," exclaimed Sakaya. She then gets up to go to the double glass door behind D's couch to look outside to see Benjamin in an effort to make eye contact with him. Eventually Benjamin looks and sees her. The feeling, as always, is electric. It's as if both of them bounce off of one another. As he was listening to the conversation between Darryn, Jarrod, and James, who were now talking about football, Benjamin walks to the double glass doors. Sakaya pushed the door to the left to open it. They kiss. Sakaya says, "It's okay, baby. I was just thinking about you and wanted to see you. You don't have to leave them." Benjamin replies, "Okay. I didn't even know that you were at the glass doors. I just looked this way. I'll see you later baby." "Okay," says Sakaya after she finally

3 YOUR WAY, OUR WAY

lets go of Benjamin's hand. He then winks at her. She blows him a kiss.

The love that they had was displayed quite well in Sakaya's book. Her book sold very well. Her author page, Twitter, Facebook, and other accounts were blowing up. The world now knew about at least one relationship, a marriage, that had a real loving connection. One that both the man and the woman were more than willing to actively participate in.

I NEED YOU, BUT WHERE DO WE GO FROM HERE?

4 SAKAYA'S STORY

A loving home of a husband and wife with a little girl. Bright eyed and full of life, Sakaya never lacked love from either parent. A strong mother, Debbie was mouthy, and by no means a pushover, and was a registered nurse at New Fountain Hospital, outside Metropola in Fortress. Her father, George, a lawyer at the Breckings Law Firm on the 3400 block Downing Street, about 10 minutes from downtown Metropola, worked long hours having a regular case load. He was a criminal lawyer who won the majority of his cases. He and Debbie would often engage in semi-heated discussions over the long hours. George also had a side business in landscaping with a friend of his, Thomas, which George and he owned. Debbie was often concerned because they both made enough money together. But George desired to one day discontinue the practice of law.

4 SAKAYA'S STORY

Sakaya went to private school, Montessori of Christ, where she achieved very good grades. The school was not far from the hospital where her mother worked. Sakaya absolutely adored her father. He would get up at night while Sakaya was sleep and change her diapers, and rock her back to sleep. He would even wash her up most nights. He was very active within his daughter's life. This is one of the many things that Debbie appreciated about him. Debbie grew up without her father being as active in her own life. It was what caused her parent's relationship to end in divorce. The one thing that she didn't like was that George didn't seem as interested in her over time.

"Good job baby. You are going to be whooping those girls and even guy's butts if they mess with you," says George.

"Thanks daddy. I'm hungry. What are we going to eat?" asks Sakaya.

"I think that we'll have takeout tonight. Tonight was a longer night for your mother. We'll get Chinese," replies George.

Sakaya was involved in a couple of extra-curricular activities including karate and playing the flute in Music at her school. The parents would alternate attending her practices. At times, they were both able to attend.

As Sakaya got older, her parents began to grow further and further apart. Sakaya heard their arguments over the years. Her father would never fuss at her mother in front of her. He would always find ways to pull Debbie to the

I NEED YOU, BUT WHERE DO WE GO FROM HERE?

side or take her into another room. Debbie would not care about where the arguments occurred. She rarely hesitated to speak her mind - even at times in public. The one good thing about Debbie, though, was that she never yelled at nor talked down to George. This would prove vitally influential later in Sakaya's life and in Sakaya's relationship with Benjamin.

At the age of 21, Sakaya's parents split up, but they remained married. After some time, George found ways to rekindle the love between Debbie and him. George had already, five years before, when Sakaya was 18, walked away from practicing law full-time. He became a legal consultant and focused on his landscaping. Debbie was pleased that George had freed up much of his time. After all, this was one of Debbie's major gripes with him. When Sakaya was 24, and done with college, had her own condo, and was married for the first time, George and Debbie got back together. It was better the second time around. Unfortunately for Sakaya, her marriage was not at all ideal for her.

Nathan, Sakaya's first husband, was quite a stand-offish person. He was also very private, bossy, demanding, and extremely selfish. He managed to hide, as much as he could, many of these negative traits. There are also things that we can still see, though, for our own reasons, we ignore them. We often impose what we want upon others, expecting them to live out or be what it is we desire. Sakaya, like the rest of us have and are probably still doing, did this in regard to Nathan.

On Tuesday, two o'clock in the afternoon, in the often dry and boring class of Economics, Nathan sat two desks to

4 SAKAYA'S STORY

the left of Sakaya, in the fourth row of desks. Both of them Juniors at Excel University, located on Excel Boulevard in Upper Metropola, Nathan secretly liked Sakaya, having talked to her from time to time, often just being friendly. He knew her through her friend Rhonda, who was more talkative and expressive than Sakaya. The time had come for Nathan to make his move.

"Hey Sakaya," offers Nathan.

"Hey Nathan," replies Sakaya.

"What are you doing Friday night?" asks Nathan.

"More than likely I'll be hanging out with Rhonda. Why?" replies Sakaya.

"Why don't you come with me to Right Burger?" asks Nathan.

"You just want me to come with you?" says Sakaya.

"Yes. Just you," offers Nathan.

"Okay. I'll come with you," answers Sakaya.

After some time, hanging out together, doing homework together, they actually began to officially date. This was the first serious relationship for the both of them. They both fell for each other so much that Nathan offered for her hand in marriage. George, after having learned of this from Sakaya, was not happy with the thought of his daughter getting mar-

I NEED YOU, BUT WHERE DO WE GO FROM HERE?

ried so soon. But he held his real feelings about it. He felt guilty for the split between Debbie and him and wondered about the impact that it may have had on Sakaya.

"Baby, I will say this. I think that you should wait at least until college is over," says George.

"Daddy, we want to wait until college is over," replies Sakaya.

Nathan was from a more affluent family than Sakaya's. His father, Sam was a neurosurgeon, and his mother, Lisa, managed her own investment firm. Nathan was just coming into his own. He was tall, 6'3", handsome, and really starting to get attention from the ladies. This did not help matters between him and Sakaya later. Both of them having finished college at the age of 21, Nathan didn't want to wait until they were 22. Debbie was happy that Sakaya was marrying someone who came from a well-to-do family and for the fact that they both attended university together. So, Debbie had no qualms about the marriage. George, while feeling guilty about their earlier split, also relented talking Sakaya out of marriage due to knowing that Debbie had no problem with it. The last thing that George wanted was there to be issues between them again.

Sadly, the marriage between Sakaya and Nathan would barely last a year. A split after six months, ended up with Sakaya moving back in with her parents. A young lady, Tanya, contacted her and told her about how Nathan and her were seeing each other, not only while they were married, but also about three months prior. Sakaya did not want to

4 SAKAYA'S STORY

go through this again with him. Things had already changed between him and her even before Tanya contacted her about the cheating. Nathan would come home late often, would barely talk to her, would not clean up, and often had an attitude with her. All of this after the first two months of their marriage! Sakaya did still try and work it out for a while. She tells Nathan about the phone call and subsequent meet-up at a department store in Lower Metropola. Nathan denies it at first. After a few minutes of listening to Sakaya's elevated voice and watching her highly expressive yet angry body language, Nathan says,

"You know what? Fuck it. I did it. So what?"

"How could you do this to me? Now I know why we weren't having sex much. The long hours at work. The coming home late. The attitude. What did I do to you?" asks Sakaya.

"Whatever. Now you know. Fuck she tell you for anyway. Fuck her too!" replies Nathan.

Nathan, while he did care about Sakaya and wanted to marry her initially, had begun to see how women were responding to him. He met Tanya three months before Sakaya and he were married. They hit it off even better than Sakaya and he had. Tanya, unaware that Nathan and Sakaya were about to get married, had sex with Nathan within the first week they were seeing each other. Tanya lived in Lower Metropola, which is 30 miles south of Metropola, the main city. Nathan had family that lived in Lower Metropola. He knew, or at least thought that he knew, that he could get away

I NEED YOU, BUT WHERE DO WE GO FROM HERE?

with it. Nathan even met other women within the same time frame. He would go see them from time to time too. Nathan eventually began seeing four women at the same time whenever he could. After a while, Sakaya would learn about some of the other women and for that it was truly the last straw. Now, 23 years old, and divorced, Sakaya focused on her career. This is about the time that she met Shanice and subsequently Sandra. Because of Sakaya's business acumen and attention to detail, she partnered with Shanice, Darryn and their business partners.

Sakaya eventually meets Benjamin at a business summit in the "Hot District," the rumbling city, located 15 miles West of Metropola, at a time when Benjamin's life was turning around for the better. After six months of dating they decide to become a couple. After an additional six months, Benjamin decided to have another conversation with Sakaya. He decided to ask for her hand in marriage. Initially Sakaya was taken aback by his request.

"Baby, don't you think it's too soon?" asks Sakaya.

"I believe that I have found what I was looking for," offers Benjamin.

"Baby, I've been married before, and we did it early. I'm not so sure I want to just yet," says Sakaya.

"I don't want to marry you and be with other people. I haven't been with anyone else since the day that you and I started seeing each other. I do what I say. I want you. If I wanted other people too, I am man enough to say that," replies Benjamin.

"I know baby, you always do what you say. I do love you. When were you thinking about doing it?" asks Sakaya.

"How about six months?" Benjamin responds.

"Okay baby," replies Sakaya.

A month later they moved in together. They discussed everything from finances, to where they wanted to live, to how many children that they desired to have. They were very open and honest with each other and maintained their chemistry between each other. The good thing that they both had beyond being lovers is that they were friends too. They actually liked doing the same things together. They shared a similar world view. They shared similar beliefs, even spiritual. Since Benjamin had taken the time to become knowledgeable on many topics, Sakaya absolutely loved that she could come to him instead of her father about most things. So, living together worked very well for them. After the six months, they were married. Sakaya ended up conceiving Sakoya the wedding night. They didn't waste any time to begin baby-making.

After about a year of marriage, Sakaya decided to write a book about their love experience. Benjamin was not comfortable at first with the world knowing about what they had. He believed that people would try and sabotage it. Sakaya was so happy that she had in her mind set to vigorously guard against infiltrators that might come about. She most definitely did not want her second marriage to end, let alone

I NEED YOU, BUT WHERE DO WE GO FROM HERE?

like her first one.

What Love Really Looks Like

Chirping birds, bright sun, a light breeze, 74 degrees, a dog is being walked by an older woman, as Sakaya sits on the bench with her notepad and pen. A man runs along the asphalt path, headphones in his ears, just before he passes a family of three walking in the opposite direction. In her long yellow dress, sandaled feet, hair pinned, she loses herself in thought about the four years that had passed since her and Benjamin were first together.

She would find time, for the most part, to write a chapter per day, or close to that. While sitting on the bench, Sakaya harkens back to her conversations with her mother, who at one time did not believe that Sakaya realistically experienced a love that was described to her. Over a process of time with Debbie also observing Benjamin's behavior and how he and Sakaya interacted, she began to encourage her daughter to open up even more to Benjamin.

"Momma, he makes me feel like what the fairy tales describes. I know we are both human and all and that fairy tales are just stories. But the way he looks at me, the way he touches me, the things that he does for me, a lot of times I feel like a little girl. He's so smart, too, momma. I find myself thinking about him all the time. I even dream about him," says Sakaya.

"Baby, your father loves me similarly. Not as deep as you're saying. But I like his love. I was so happy when he left the law firm. We go almost everywhere together now. He never objected to you being with Benjamin. I think I see why now. I'm glad that you're happy. I no longer have any doubts that you two will be just fine," replies Debbie.

After a few months of writing about her experiences being with Benjamin, Sakaya began typing up her book. After editing, proofreading, and layout, she had a freelance book designer design a cover for her book. Then off to editorial reviews. She then hired a local marketing and promotion agent to get eyes on her book. Her book was well received by most women and even some men. There were, however, some women who did not receive it well, due to the fact of their own relationship failures as well as being unable to believe that such a thing could take place. This in no way stopped Sakaya from pressing forward. Benjamin encouraged her throughout the process and was pleased to read some things that she had not even shared with him directly. This would cause him to be drawn even more towards her, and she to him. It took a matter of eight months for "What Love Really Looks Like" to become a best seller.

I NEED YOU, BUT WHERE DO WE GO FROM HERE?

5 WHERE WE ARE

At a time where the relationship between men and women is much more adversarial, at least in general, men and women need each other now more than ever. After having been married for a long time, and maintaining a few relationships leading to marriage and afterwards, I had come to the conclusion that life without love leaves a horrible feeling and taste in one's mouth. It has been outlined how we got to where we are as demonstrated above. A window into how things are from different perspectives has, too been demonstrated above. There is no one way when it comes to male and female relationships nor intersexual dynamics. The world is full of grey. After much research, I had found that monogamy, polygamy, and other forms of pair bonding have always existed. The individuals determine what they want if not dictated by culture, society, etc. Even a cursory reading into ancient history demonstrates the different forms of pair bonding.

5 WHERE WE ARE

Some relationships begin with a natural chemistry. That chemistry can remain, if properly maintained, or it can dissolve altogether regardless of whether it was the man or the woman that caused it to do so. I have found, generally, that the health of a relationship is largely determined upon how often the partners are having sexual intercourse. There are some people who do not see sex as important, or as important as it truly is. It is a great thing to find a partner from the opposite sex that you can enjoy hobbies and get along very well with. However, there is the one thing that the opposite sex can provide that our own sex and even ourselves cannot provide us with. It is also true that love and sex are not synonymous. Sometimes people desire to have sex just for the act, whether male or female. So, if a man and a woman join themselves in a relationship, it only makes sense that while they are attracted to one another, the sexual arousal component is more than likely there as well. Otherwise, that relationship is platonic and should more than likely just be a friendship. At the end of the day, people are going to do what they desire to do, except where the environment and opportunity dictates otherwise.

The Male Response to Female Freedom

After the many changes that took place from the 1960s moving forward, women have been on the rise economically, financially, socially, mentally, etc. Many women today are in no need of male provision. With the shift in thought, in general, women are no longer held to the stringent standards of being seen as less than for not being married. There are many women who also are enjoying multiple sex partners, and this too, is not looked down upon within our modern society. The education of male and female children in this regard has been on different sides of the spectrum. Men were, and still are, seen in a good light if they are the type that can bed many women. While the stigma for women doing the same is not looked down upon as in the past, there are still a number of men and women who do tend to not look at it in positive ways. I would say that men and women should have the freedom to do what they choose and not be judged. But it is true that depending upon what one desires to do, they should consider the very real and possible consequences that may and often does come. With there being an estimated 7.5 billion people in the world, what one desires in a partner is available. That person just may have to drive or fly to another city, state, and even country to find it. This too, goes on far more than many may be aware of. The so-called traditional way of looking at things, as we have already dealt with in relation to marriage above, is not as widely held as it once was.

While there are a number of men who are celebrating the rise of women and what is now available to them, there are still quite a few men who very much have a problem with how things are panning out now.[52] Some of these men, and there are women too, have been termed as trad-cons, or traditional conservatives. Many of them want things back to what they believe they were. What many fail to realize is that we generally romanticize the past as though all things, or at least most, was so much better than today. This is not necessarily the case. We tend to look back or forward from our own time due to challenges and other things that we do not like about our own time. Prior to the 1950s, the marriag-

---

52   (H. Smith 1), (H. Smith 12)

5 WHERE WE ARE

es and overall scene of monogamy was not as rosy as many would like to believe. There were many marriages and families formed out of necessity. This does not mean that love was not a part of the equation. But love alone, like many other things alone, is not enough. Freedom is more available now, and as stated above, with freedom comes responsibility. The more of a positive thing that you receive, comes a greater possibility of losing it if accountability is not taken into consideration.

As in all things, there seems to be a constant balancing act going on. When one thing rises, an opposition against it rises. As Feminism empowered women, and seemingly lowered men or caused men and women to swap places from a class perspective, male movements began to rise up. From about the year 2000, what has been termed the Manosphere,[iii] has rose up where some groups within there were more alpha-minded men beginning to educate, so to speak, the more beta-minded men. Alpha and beta, along with other concepts are more like placeholders. They are mindsets and not demographics as rightly stated by Rollo Tomassi. It is a mindset that you either developed or it came to you naturally.[53] The behavior of anyone is a result of their mindset. As stated before, I agree with Rollo Tomassi where he states that our personalities are malleable and not static.[54] Alan Roger Currie in his, *The Beta Male Revolution: Why Men Have Totally Lost Interest in Marriage in Today's Society*, discusses the alpha and beta traits in a way that I have not seen expressly done. The point is that these terms are placeholders, as stated by Rollo Tomassi. They are not

---

53   (Tomassi, Defining Alpha 27)
54   (Tomassi, Just Be Yourself: We are who we say we are 125)

I NEED YOU, BUT WHERE DO WE GO FROM HERE?

straitjackets. Alphas are more successful with women as well as successful with men, who desire to be like them and follow them. There are levels to this just like with anything else. So, the Manosphere in general exists to assist men in many ways to becoming better. There are some Manosphere groups that aid in the division of the sexes. This makes sense when one considers the legal aspect. However, the truth is, as stated before, that men and women are far stronger together than apart. Without one another working together, our society moving forward will become more antagonistic and negative overall. Regardless of the pain, frustration, and failure, men and women still get up after falling from bad relationship experiences and march right into another one due to our needs and longings for those things that we are unable to do on our own.[55]

Relationship and Marital Equity

Equity within the home is another concept that has been considered by the Western nations.[56] From proponents of the gender revolution theory, it has been theorized that equity within the home will provide us with a happier future with a new family model that will involve higher fertility and more stable unions. Some have even posited that women feel more warmth and affection towards their men, and provide them with more sex.[57] Others hold a different opinion on this matter. Apparently, the divorce rate among households where the married couples share the housework was as high as 50 percent more than the households that involved the wife do-

---

55 (Cowan & Kinder 120)

56 (Vitali and Berrington)

57 (Mundy, Eight: Sex and the Self-Sufficient Girl 169)

5 WHERE WE ARE

ing most of the housework.⁵⁸ Who would have thought that the more that a man does in the home, the greater risk of his marital failure, especially since many women are on record for stating that they desire that the husband does more within the home? Just because she complains doesn't mean that she wants the man to concede and change what he's doing. It would perhaps be greater that the man took care of the larger jobs that would require his natural strength, which is generally greater than the average woman. What I have found is that if a man stands his ground and does not mind his woman being upset, she will respect him more in the long run.

Regarding the Social Contract

A concept unknown to some is that of the social contract.⁵⁹ For more than two centuries, the American dream, *"... a belief in a society characterized by political and religious freedom in which anyone, regardless of family background, ethnicity, or race, can "make it." By making it, we mean that people can—by virtue of education, hard work, luck, and motivation—have a good job, a home, a happy family, and leisure time. Moreover, they can have these in a social climate free from oppression,"*⁶⁰ has been a central

---

58 (Samuel), ("Roissy", Chateau Heartiste: Where Pretty Lies Perish), (Thomas Hansen 223-228)

59 Social contract - An implicit agreement among the members of a society to cooperate for social benefits, for example by sacrificing some individual freedom for state protection. Theories of a social contract became popular in the 16th, 17th, and 18th centuries among theorists such as Thomas Hobbes, John Locke, and Jean-Jacques Rousseau, as a means of explaining the origin of government and the obligations of subjects. (Oxford Univeristy Press, social contract, n.1)

60 (Rubin, The American Dream 7-8) "Republished with permission of SAGE Publications, Inc., from Shifts in the Social Contract Un-

I NEED YOU, BUT WHERE DO WE GO FROM HERE?

part of our culture. Many still hold this dream very dear to their hearts, which has caused many to come from other nations to here in order to work to obtain it. There have been quite a few changes in regard to the social contract for quite some time. These changes have not only affected the economy, the government, but they have also affected family life.[61] With these many changes, it would seem as though continual or constant change has become the norm. The social contract itself has changed, specifically within the last 5 to 6 decades. Though these changes did not happen overnight, they happened under the watch of the public. As a result, we bear some of the responsibility for allowing such changes.[62]

Enormous changes took place after World War II. Women took on jobs that were left by the men who went to war. Upon returning home from war, many of those jobs were given back to the men. Later women fought for their right to work, those who were not married due to the breadwinner-female homemaker model. This model, *"... dominated the middle class was now a possibility for large portions of the working class as well. In 1940, 70% of families were male breadwinner-female homemaker families. For the next 25 years, more than half of all families conformed to this*

---

derstanding Change in American Society, Beth A. Rubin, 1996; permission conveyed through Copyright Clearance Center, Inc. "
61   (Rubin, Society in Transition 4)
62   (Blau 18)

5 WHERE WE ARE

norm."[63,64] This model worked due to there being clearly delineated gender roles. Those clearly delineated gender roles would altogether break down over time as we neared the Civil Rights era. Additionally, between the ages of 25 and 64, paid work skyrocketed for women within the workforce during the postwar economy. Alongside this trend came a male flight from work that has been largely ignored. Many men after some time decided to just stop looking for work altogether. This did not help the family situation. Mrs. Rosin seems right within her analysis of the end of men and the rise of women. With more and more men leaving the workforce, and more and more women taking the positions, it seems that a matriarchy has formed leaving the women to become the decision makers.[65]

One of the major differences that shifted the social contract was the relationship between the government and commerce. More and more political power shifted from the nation-state to the global corporations.[66] To accompany this trend, *"Since the end of the twentieth century, the United States has witnessed an ominous and growing divergence among three trends that should ordinarily move together: <u>wealth, output</u>, and employment."*[67] With family life now

63   (Rubin, Marriage, Family, and a House in the Suburbs 12) "Republished with permission of SAGE Publications, Inc., from Shifts in the Social Contract Understanding Change in American Society, Beth A. Rubin, 1996; permission conveyed through Copyright Clearance Center, Inc. "
64   (Eberstadt, Chapter 3: Postwar America's Great Male Flight from Work 33)
65   (Rosin, Introduction, 2012, p. 5)
66   (Rifkin 237)
67   (Eberstadt, Chapter 1: The Collapse of Work in the Second Gilded Age 9)

I NEED YOU, BUT WHERE DO WE GO FROM HERE?

far different than before, women outpacing men in college, in many areas within the workforce, and doing better socially, work rates for men between the early 1950s and today have plummeted by more than eighteen percentage points.[68]

The underlying winds of change began as early as the 1950s in regard to the family. Marriage was greatly affected by the changes. Personal fulfillment and sexual satisfaction had become the primary focus within marriage even as early as the 1920s. Many of these expectations, which were sought to be fulfilled within the home, seemed quite unrealistic.[69] It is generally true that it is difficult to find everything you need and desire in one person. This is one of the main reasons why men and women, over the years have developed sexual strategies to ensure that they are successful in obtaining "it all." The truth is that no one can have it all, and if so, that is a relatively small percentage of people who may even remotely come close to such a "reality."

Fertility and Hookup Culture

It seems that the more that women become educated, the less offspring they have. The more a woman focuses on her career, it not only can typically delay childbirth, but it can also typically delay family formation. Women, as they become more educated and more affluent, desire higher status men. After some time, women began to separate sex from childbirth. This was a benefit of the introduction of the birth control pill. Births began to decline after 1970, with 60 per-

---

68   (Eberstadt, Chapter 1: The Collapse of Work in the Second Gilded Age 17)

69   (Coontz, Chapter 15: Winds of Change: Marriage in the 1960s and 1970s 250)

5 WHERE WE ARE

cent of all adult women, whether married or not, using the birth control pill. To include the impact of employment and how women no longer needed men for financial security, and with sex outside of marriage no longer having the social stigma it once had, sex is now cheap.[70] With cheap sex, more people having it, and the fact that the birth control pill and other methods of contraception exist, the landscape for family formation has altogether changed.[71] Though the stigma for single mothers has been lifted, largely, women who have no children are seen as at the top of their game, depending upon their age. Problems began to develop early when marriage broke down from as early as the 1950s and 1960s. This was even apparent from the opinions of social scientists.[72] Due to the breakdown of the traditional family structure, children became much more likely to engage in not only premarital sex, but also premarital births. With the divorce rates having risen, and more and more children having become step-children, this is perhaps one of the main reasons that the stigma of premarital births having lessened, since whether born out-of-wedlock or not, a single parent is a single parent. As early as the 1990s, when the focus on the changes within the family seemed to have become much larger in focus, marriages seemed to no longer remain intact for the sake of the children. We are now in a situation where just over half of the annually contracted marriages will end in divorce.[73]

As stated above, the introduction of one thing brings

---

70   (H. Rosin 39)
71   (Douglas 66)
72   (Smith 14)
73   (Smith 21)

I NEED YOU, BUT WHERE DO WE GO FROM HERE?

along challenges to that one thing.[74] With the modern dating scene, not many are finding love and lifelong commitment. A statement made by Rollo Tomassi within a tweet, *"Women see men as breeding stock or draft animals,"* no matter how offensive is not far off from what Rosin stated, *"Men are divided into what the college girls call the players (a smaller group) and the losers (a much larger group), and the women are left fighting for small spoils. The players are in high demand and hard to pin down. The losers are not all that enticing. Neither is in any hurry to settle down."*[75] While men place women into categories, women also place men into categories. There is nothing inherently wrong about this. We are attracted to what we are attracted to, and we are sexually aroused by whom we are sexually aroused by. There is no amount of intellectualizing that one can do to get someone to find them attractive or become sexually aroused by. This is something that is instinctual. You cannot reason someone into bed. Even if you could, the sex would not be as good as it would be with someone that you have the natural animal arousal for. As often as we see that guy who goes for the type of women that he goes for, and that woman who goes for the type of men that she goes for, it is not hard to understand from an evolutionary standpoint, nor from the standpoint of the concept of sexual imprinting. It is also true that culture, and social mores can affect the sexual choices of an individual by way of conditioning. One might be surprised, though, if they saw what some men and women go for behind closed doors that they never would publicly. At the end of the day, men and women do the same things but for different reasons, while going about what they

---

74   (Pinker, 2002, pp. 10-11)
75   (H. Rosin 38)

5 WHERE WE ARE

do in different ways.

I NEED YOU, BUT WHERE DO WE GO FROM HERE?

6 WHAT HAPPENS NOW?

What happens now? What do we do moving forward? With all of the technological changes in regard to work, the changes within the economy, finance, and business, they are affecting us on many levels of everyday life. How we are able to eat, pay bills, and date, is altogether moving in different directions that are forcing us to find craftier methods in order to do so. From a long denial of human nature by some over the years, it seems that the acceptance of it is peering back into view. People, in general, do what they choose except where the environment and circumstances dictate otherwise. There has also been a long-time debate concerning perception and reality. Some deny reality altogether. By reality, I mean observable reality. Perception has to do with how a person sees observable reality which is shaped by their past experiences. At least largely. I see what appears to be a constant balancing going on from various aspects of life, where the forces of "good"

6 WHAT HAPPENS NOW?

and the forces of "evil" are always at work, alongside one another.

Marriage Moving Forward

Even with the apparent ups and downs of marriage, people are clearly still marrying. The landscape is changing, though, with as of 2001, 81 percent of more affluent families with children were headed by married couples.[76] With poverty being one of the major factors as to whether a marriage takes place, it seems as though the more affluent and skilled are going to be the most married in the future. Whether this has to do with social status or class, the day may come where if you are not within a certain income bracket, you may never walk down the aisle at all.

Childbearing is different when you compare poor families to more affluent families. The poor families have more children than the more affluent families. Since the poor are less married, the number of children being born to unwed parents has risen over time. The fathers to these children are much more likely to be imprisoned or jailed, lack a high school education, and to not have a job.[77] This matters little to some, but it does matter when it comes to demography, seeing how developing countries has a projected need of 2.1 Total Fertility Rate (TFR) in order to replace those that are retiring and others who are dying.[78] Over a course of a woman's years, the Total Fertility Rate represents the average number of children that she will bear. The TFR is currently, as a magic number in demography, what has been

76 (Haskins and Sawhill 2)
77 (Kathryn Edin, Introduction 2)
78 (World Health Organization), (Wattenberg 12)

I NEED YOU, BUT WHERE DO WE GO FROM HERE?

termed the replacement level. It is explained that if two children plus one-tenth of a child must be given birth to by the average woman, despite other factors not being explained, in order to survive the parents or the population will decline over time. The next few generations will look quite interesting depending upon where the pendulum swings in regard to family formation.

The Need For Control

Control is very important and is at times on the forefront of the minds of many a man or woman. Now that more and more women are working, it is paramount for some within their relationships. Many women feel as if having their own money buys them more say within their relationships. So, if the man decides to act differently, a woman with her own money can pick up and leave if she so chooses. This is incredibly important within the context of the cohabitation model. Some feel as if this desire for economic independence comes from a fear that no matter how good the relationship or marriage is, it will at some point head for the worse.[79]

As stated above, instead of marriage, many couples are cohabitating. Cohabitation for some is a far better deal. It gives the sense of less expectations and the fact that either party could walk away at any time. While either party is not obligated to stay within a cohabitating situation, marriage does not guarantee that either partner will remain. For some, cohabitation is not as ideal as it might be for others. One particular case where cohabitation may not be ideal for some is

---

79   (Kathryn Edin, Introduction 8-9)

6 WHAT HAPPENS NOW?

the case of sexual fidelity. When better options for sex and even partners to cohabit with come along, this is important for those who are looking for a better arrangement.[80] Truth be told, marriage does not insulate one from sex outside of the marriage nor does it alleviate one from divorcing and jumping upon another opportunity to find a better spouse. Marriage more so gives the peace of mind that these things will more than likely not happen and offers barriers, i.e. legal, against doing so as fast as would a cohabitating situation would allow. Though marriage and the views toward it has changed quite a bit over time, there are still those that see marriage as very important and even pedestalize it until this day.

From what I have come to understand, control is important to those who have fears that things will not go their way. Whether it is the man or the woman, control and/or dominance exist to make up for what one has at some point in time lacked. This individual has no desire to lack what they have at one time any longer. Some control and dominate openly, while others have a much more subtle way of doing so. At the end of the day, fear should be dealt with from an individual place, or that individual needs to go and seek help. The truth is, in a world where certain levels of control are not possible, perhaps we should come to accept that we are not as in control as we would like to allow ourselves to believe. It is hard when it comes to feelings. No one wants to get hurt. So, men and women develop tactics in an effort to still have certain experiences while mitigating the possibility of feeling pain as much as possible. The problem is that no one can gauge pain in one way or another. If we go into a

---

80   (Kathryn Edin, 3. How Does the Dream Die? 79-80)

I NEED YOU, BUT WHERE DO WE GO FROM HERE?

relationship expecting failure or failings, we will more than likely experience the effects of such failure or failings. This is when one might want to look in the mirror and realize their own failure or failings. It is probably not a good idea to expect perfection when we ourselves are not perfect.

Mate Access

Assortative mating has become a major focus within modern society. Many men and women desire to have a mate that is similar to them in education, social status, personality, looks, etc. There are levels within society just as anything else. Depending upon where one fits socially will determine, generally, what access to particular mates they will have. Those that are less educated, earn less income, will typically not have access to mates that are more educated and who earn more in income. People want others who are similar to themselves when it comes to mates, though they may have sexual encounters across a broader spectrum. This implies that mate priority and sexual priority are not synonymous. This implication would prove correct, at least generally. From time to time, though, men and women still get together and become couples whether it is in a cohabitating situation or marriage despite the barriers.

Out-of-Wedlock Births and No More Shotgun Marriage

Out-of-wedlock births are of major concern and were dealt with differently in the past. This topic concerns the next generation far more than many seem to realize. Children who are born in unmarried homes are much likely to end up in poverty, poor health, drop out of school, impris-

6 WHAT HAPPENS NOW?

oned or jailed, and some committed to a mental institution.[81] This not only affects children who are born into unmarried households but this also affects children who are born into married households that end in divorce. Due to a change in sexual behavior, and one could argue the views toward romantic relationships, single parenthood has increased since the 1960s. Prior to the early 1970s, the practice of the shotgun marriage, where the unwed partners would marry in the event of pregnancy, was the norm. With the rise of contraceptives and abortion, the practice of shotgun marriage became a thing of the past. These technological tools shifted the focus of family formation to the woman. Now a woman can choose whether to have the baby or not. After some time, men began to catch on that they no longer had to commit to marriage in order to have sex, with willing women being partners with them, some due to fear of losing access to the man. So, contraception, abortion, and women willing to have sex with men due to fear of losing them has been some of the main contributory factors to the structural changes in regard to the family.

Once this paradigm shift was fully set in, single motherhood began to be approached differently. Women are fully in the driver's seat now and no longer face the stigma that they once faced. In 1969, 28 percent of children of unmarried mothers were kept after three years, 56 percent in 1984, and 66 percent in the 1980s.[82] This implies that over time, women became more willing to keep the children whether the man would want to marry them or even be a part of the

---

81 (J. L. George A. Akerlof 278), (Christensen, Preface), (Kathryn Edin, Introduction 3)
82 (J. L. George A. Akerlof)

I NEED YOU, BUT WHERE DO WE GO FROM HERE?

rearing of the child or not. With this in mind, women have proven that they are going to have babies no matter what. As a consequence of this reality, the social policies were suggested by certain organizations to make it costly for the fathers of the children. In other words, the responsibility for the children have been placed within the laps of the fathers fiscally. This fiscal component could be seen as a way, over time, to help men realize that they are the ones that need to be more sexually responsible and perhaps start saying no. Theory and practice do not always coincide. There are not a few men that are going to continue impregnating women, and have done, whether they plan on marrying them or taking on active roles within the children's' lives.

Social Implications and the Family Moving Forward

It has been rightly observed by some that the social environment not only forms human personality, but is itself made up largely of the personalities that it has created.[83] Even the immediate physical surroundings, social relationships, and cultural milieus are encompassed by human social environments.[84] The cultural and social changes from the 1970s moving forward have had significant impact upon the family structure. This was not only observed within the United States, but also in Europe, where marriage and childbirth began to be postponed while cohabitation and out-of-wedlock births began to increase.[85] With marriages and childbirth within them lessening, and cohabitation and out-of-wedlock births on the rise, this would cause a subsequent reduction

---

83 (Quigley, Man and Culture 57)
84 (M. C. Elizabeth Barnett)
85 (Vitali and Berrington)

6 WHAT HAPPENS NOW?

in the birthrate. It is well known that it is expensive to raise a child. It is far more expensive to raise a child as a single parent. So, low income is one of the main reasons why fewer children are being born. Another reason is due to the fact that the more educated women become, the less children they bear as well. Now married families form less often and much later in life.[86] With women working more and men working less, women more educated and men less educated, marriages are becoming more and more rare and for primarily higher earning men and women. These higher-earning women who are marrying are demanding more out of their husbands in regard to helping out with the children and work around the home. This hearkens back the egalitarian model spoken of above. The experts are mixed on whether this will work moving forward or not. We will see in time. As far as the social implications, as I stated above, communities are made of families. How strong or weak those families are will determine the strength or weakness of those communities. So, where might we be headed?

It is clear that prior to the changes of the 1960s and later, things were not perfect. It was not good that women were controlled by society and men had more freedom. The old model was not perfect by any stretch of the imagination. The movements of the 1960s and later brought much more freedom and many social changes. We are, however, again in a place where things are not perfect. It is clear that in moving forward, family is the key. Whether that family is actually in a contractual marriage or in a cohabitating situation, the family is altogether too important for the furthering of society. It is well documented and undeniable that children need

---

86   (U.S. Census Bureau)

I NEED YOU, BUT WHERE DO WE GO FROM HERE?

both parents in their rearing if they are to be more successful than not as opposed to children who are reared by single parents. It is true that not all single parent homes contribute to the negative statistics that we are aware of in regard to education, employment, and becoming an overall productive member of society. But it is categorically, demonstrably, and verifiably true that a two-parent home is generally better than a single parent home. In an ideal world, the person that we fall in love with, sleep with, could become our spouse, if that's what we want, and we live happily ever after. Reality has yet to reflect this to the entirety or totality of the average persons experience. This just is generally not the case.

Perhaps we should teach our children early on about sex, friendships, relationships, etc. Maybe we shouldn't sugar-coat our teachings, and give our children as much truth as they can handle depending upon whether we are able to properly gauge their maturity at any given point and time. The world can be a harsh place at times. The more we are armed with the knowledge about how the real world works as opposed to focusing on what we want out of the world, solely, the better off we might become.

Honesty and forwardness are not something that all people are able and or willing to utilize in their dealings with the opposite sex. Due to our own individual fears and failings, we often tend to lie, desire to control, manipulate, and use other tactics to protect our feelings while still actively seeking what we desire. The problem is that this rarely, if at all, ever works. I have learned that how you deal with others, opens the door for them to deal with you the same way. This is what I got years ago from a statement made by Jesus,

6 WHAT HAPPENS NOW?

And as ye would that men should do to you, do ye also to them likewise.

Luke 6:31 KJV

What I took from this is that you do not dish out what you cannot take, as well as if you do not want it done to you then do not do it to someone else. In an ideal world, this would be a common reality. But in this world, whosever ideals it is based upon, this rarely happens. Or it has not happened as much as I would like to have seen it. The truth is we are all dysfunctional somewhere. Admitting to ourselves and choosing to deal with the dysfunction(s) in healthy ways would be best. This is what I think that we should keep in mind when it comes to dealing with each other within our relationships, romantic or otherwise.

If we do not stop pointing the finger at others and sit down and find better solutions as to how to deal with how things are currently in regard to family and relationships, then things will only get worse. We all have opinions that have come from our own individual experiences and what we have learned through others as well as through study. Our culture and society have been in flux for quite some time. Change takes time, but the sooner we get started the better. Romantic relationships are up to the two parties that are involved. They should be open and honest with one another about what they think and feel. We should not be trying to get over on one another. There is nothing like finding out you were duped later, or yielding to someone and realizing by that yielding how far they were willing to go in damaging you. Though you allowed it.

I NEED YOU, BUT WHERE DO WE GO FROM HERE?

CONCLUSION

Love is a beautiful thing and it is great when one finds it, or think that they have. Regardless, when you have those feelings, when that chemistry is so strong, it is as if nothing else matters. I have had the privilege of experiencing that feeling more than once. For a time while with the woman that I experienced that feeling with, it temporarily made the past pain of no consequence. After having experienced it a few times, it became apparent to me that this feeling, or at least I, could be controlled. It didn't have to go so far as to cause you to make certain decisions during the feeling that you would have otherwise not made, and later regretted when the relationship for whatever reason went south. Men and women are far stronger and better together than apart. So, yes, we do need each other. When you take the necessity out of the equation, there really is no relationship. That is commonly termed today, a situationship. The term situationship has been given, at least as far

CONCLUSION

as I have seen, to some modern relationships which only last on average two to six months. This is in no way sustainable long-term.

It is not at all clear at this time what is to be done about the male situation in regard to employment nor college. More and more men since the end of World War II have been dropping out of the labor force. Women began to take on more jobs near that time. With more men not actively seeking work, this drains the pool of potential and available mates overall from the male population. Simply telling men to be motivated or man up is not going to work. As stated above, human beings are driven by incentive. With no incentive, people will do little to nothing. Perhaps there are policies in place or are being written by the thinktanks within this nation that are going to address this issue more readily, as Nicholas Eberstadt has done in his *Men Without Work: America's Invisible Crisis.*

It is true that women have been schooled more as girls than men as boys long before the 1950s. This holds true today. However, jobs were more readily available for men prior to World War II. Many of these did not require obtaining a college degree. This is not the case as it once was. More and more women are attending and graduating college than men, depending upon the particular college, at an alarming rate.[87] This places women in a more powerful economic position in general. I have talked with some women who are not at all comfortable with settling down with a man that doesn't make as much as them, and some if not more. That pool of

---

87 (H. Smith, Chapter 3: The College Strike: Where the Boys Aren't 83-84)

I NEED YOU, BUT WHERE DO WE GO FROM HERE?

available men has shrunk overall. Now with Title IX, Title X, the *"Dear Colleague Letter,"*[88] and the college climate that some have posited to be anti-male, the college rates for men will more than likely drop even more. This anti-male behavior was not just posited in regard to college, but even at the grade school level by others.[89] This has not and is not heading within a good direction.

Women seem to hold the cards now. It is as if the roles and even positions have been altogether shifted. While women are rising, men are indeed falling, or ending, as Hanna Rosin has stated. Men and women are stronger together. But with the liberation of women seems to have come the restriction of men. Some have posited that the sexuality and freedom of men is now being controlled. The past continues with the positions reversed, or so it seems.[90]

While there is a number of women who are indeed critical and even outright hateful towards men, there are still plenty of women who actually like and even love men. Unfortunately, the climate as it stands currently is causing the women who desire healthy relationships and even marriage with men to lose out.[91] It is already bad enough that women outnumber men and even more so in larger cities.[92] One thing that the women who actually like and love men

---

88   (OFFICE OF THE ASSISTANT SECRETARY), (H. Smith, Chapter 3: The College Strike: Where the Boys Aren't 90-91)
89   (H. Smith, Chapter 3: The College Strike: Where the Boys Aren't 69-70)
90   (H. Smith, Chapter 3: The College Strike: Where the Boys Aren't 93)
91   (H. Smith, Chapter 5: Why it Matters 134)
92   (Connell Cowan 104)

CONCLUSION

might consider is perhaps find the places where they think good men hang out at. The way things seem to be going, a time may come where the woman may have to do more approaching and making herself more available. More and more men in some places are making themselves far scarcer due to an environment that is seemingly growing more and more anti-male.

We have seen a brief sketch of how we got here and where we are. Where are we going? Well that question can really only be answered by all of us coming together, being open and honest, and deciding to actively find solutions for what has become of the many changes over the past few decades. Our children are important because they are our future. Some of us who are adults understand this all too well. How many of us have looked back and wished that we not only had done differently, but that perhaps our parents and extended family should have as well? I don't have all of the answers any more than anyone else does. But if we come together to discuss this in an open and honest way, we will have those answers together. I want us to be the best that we can be. This best begins, but doesn't end, in the home. Growing up is a life long process of development. The truth is that no matter how great your parents are, the quest for perfection never ends. But it is most important how we are reared within the home in our early years of development. May we either get back to a place, or get to a place where we make this our priority, which first begins with a strong husband/father and wife/mother. I am by no means excluding unmarried fathers and mothers who decide to cohabit.

I NEED YOU, BUT WHERE DO WE GO FROM HERE?

SURVEY QUESTIONS

During the research stages of the current work, we conducted a survey in order to get a first hand idea of where men and women stood. Below is a copy of the survey questions. We will later utilize our results in order to complete a commentary.

Purpose of Questionnaire: We at Intelligent Publishing are currently working on a project that involves the writing and research for exploring the modern dating marketplace from a married and non-married perspective. We desire to learn this information so that within our findings, we will incorporate information that we utilize to inform those who desire to participate and later read (after having conducted our findings we will incorporate them into reports and a book), what we compile from our evidence. We would very much appreciate it if you were to aid us in our findings that we may produce for those who desire to read it, the best and most informative and well written documentation. We also do indeed hope that when we are finished with our final products that the readers will be well equipped to know what they can do to win in today's dating marketplace.

Name: (Optional)

Gender: M / F

Age Range: 16-24 25-33 34-42 43-51 52-60

SURVEY QUESTIONS

Locality: Region 1: Northeast[93] Region 2: Midwest[94]
Region 3: South[95]   Region 4: West[96]

Questions: Please answer the following questions as best and truthful as you can. The purpose of these questions is to solicit answers that will help us get an idea of what those who are married or non-married think about the modern dating scene, and how they feel about it, whether it is a positive or negative environment. We understand that the dating marketplace is different in different parts of the country, which is why we ask you to give us an idea of where you live. We desire to receive this information from people directly instead of going by popular surveys and studies, whether scholarly or mainstream. In answering these questions, please feel free to elaborate and don't feel like you're being too wordy if you so choose. If there are some questions that you are not comfortable with, feel free to leave them blank.

1.   How do you feel about the modern dating scene in
_____

---

[93]   Division 1: New England (Connecticut, Maine, Massachusetts, New Hampshire, Rhode Island, and Vermont) Division 2: Mid-Atlantic (New Jersey, New York, and Pennsylvania)

[94]   Division 3: East North Central (Illinois, Indiana, Michigan, Ohio, and Wisconsin) Division 4: West North Central (Iowa, Kansas, Minnesota, Missouri, Nebraska, North Dakota, and South Dakota)

[95]   Division 5: South Atlantic (Delaware, Florida, Georgia, Maryland, North Carolina, South Carolina, Virginia, District of Columbia, and West Virginia) Division 6: East South Central (Alabama, Kentucky, Mississippi, and Tennessee) Division 7: West South Central (Arkansas, Louisiana, Oklahoma, and Texas)

[96]   Division 8: Mountain (Arizona, Colorado, Idaho, Montana, Nevada, New Mexico, Utah, and Wyoming) Division 9: Pacific (Alaska, California, Hawaii, Oregon, and Washington) (Wikipedia, List of regions of the United States)

I NEED YOU, BUT WHERE DO WE GO FROM HERE?

general?

2. Have you ever heard of Assortative Mating?[97] What are your thoughts on it?

3. Would you rather haven lived in the past such as the 1960s, 70s, 80s, etc., or do you feel that now is better in regard to dating?

4. How do you feel about family values and are they any different today as opposed to years past?

5. Are you open to traveling to find a mate? Would you move to that place whether it is another state or country, or would you rather have them move to where you are?

6. How important is college education in your mate?

7. How much money do you desire your mate to make, more, the same, or more than you?

8. Do you desire marriage?

9. Do you desire to have children?

10. Would you be open to cohabitating with someone?

11. Would you have a problem being the breadwinner in your marriage/cohabitation arrangement?

---

[97] People who "… pair off and marry someone who is very similar to themselves – similar levels of education, physical attractiveness, height, weight etc." (CORDIS, 2017)

ABOUT THE AUTHOR

Benjamin Samuel Brasford lived a relatively normal life, though, went through some major changes and battles in the beginning stages of his adulthood. After having been involved in an arranged marriage for a long time, he finally was able to free himself and begin to live life on his own terms. During the latter five years of his marriage, he began doing research in an effort to learn about and understand life, beginning from where he was mentally at the time - Christianity. The Christian studies led to several others topics to include metaphysics, atheism, sociology, biology, anthropology, archaeology, ancient and modern history, economics, business, and cultural diversity. After the years of time, effort, situations, and application, Benjamin began writing about what he had learned with a desire to assist others in their journey. Benjamin will continue learning, exploring and writing in the future on many of these same subject matters, as well as others not expressly stated within the current work. Please feel free to visit the following links, if you desire to follow Benjamin to remain aware of his current and future developments.

Blog: https://theworkseries.com/

Twitter: https://twitter.com/Brasford17

Academic:https://independent.academia.edu/Benjamin-Brasford

This page intentionally left blank

Endnotes

i   The Work Volume I: The Life of Benjamin Samuel Brasford. The Work Volume II: Transformation.

ii   See "College Education and Dating and Mating," at: https://www.academia.edu/38307209/College_Education_and_Dating_Mating

iii The manosphere is an informal network where commentators and blogs, forums[1] and websites, some seen as men's spaces, focus on issues relating to men and masculinity. It is also seen by some as a male counterpart to feminism or in opposition to it.

The content of manosphere articles varies widely. Common topics include antifeminism, fathers' rights, incels,[2][3] Men Going Their Own Way (MGTOW) movements, men's rights, male victims of abuse,[4] and pick-up artistry[1][4] and self-improvement.[5] Prominent websites in the manosphere include Chateau Heartiste,[6] Return of Kings,[7] and SlutHate(formerly PUAHate).[1][8][9] (Wikipedia, Manosphere)

Works Cited

"Roissy", Chateau Heartiste. "Chateau Heartiste: Where Pretty Lies Perish." 29 September 2012. Don't Split The Housework If You Want The Love To Last. <https://heartiste.wordpress.com/2012/09/29/dont-split-the-housework-if-you-want-the-love-to-last/>.

""'The Retreat From Marriage': Summary of a Discussion." The Retreat From Marriage: Causes and Consequences. Ed. Bryce J. Christensen. Lanham: University of America Press, Inc., 1990. 99-162. Book.

American Sociological Association. "Women more likely than men to initiate divorces, but not non-marital break-ups." 22 August 2015. ScienceDaily. ScienceDaily. <www.sciencedaily.com/releases/2015/08/150822154900.htm>.

Blau, Judith R. "2 Tumbling toward Two Thousand." Blau, Judith R. Social Contracts and Economic Markets. New York, London: Plenum Press, 1993. 17-18. Book.

Britannica, The Editors of Encyclopaedia. "Assortative mating." 1 June 2012. Encyclopædia Britannica. Website. 27 August 2018. <https://www.britannica.com/science/assortative-mating>.

Carnevale, Anthony P., Nicole Smith and Artem Gulish. "Women Can't Win." 27 February 2018. Georgetown CEW. Publication. 29 August 2018. <https://1gyhoq479ufd3yna29x7ubjn-wpengine.netdna-ssl.com/wp-content/uploads/Women_FR_Web.pdf>.

Christensen, Bryce J. "Preface." The Retreat From Marriage: Causes and Consequences. Ed. Bryce J. Christensen. Lanham: University of America Press, Inc., 1990. ix-x. Book.

Cowan, Connell & Kinder, Melvyn. "2 Getting Smart: Chapter Seven: Many Special Women, Few Good Men?" Connell Cowan, Melvyn Kinder. Smart Women, Foolish Choices: Finding The RIght Men and Avoiding the Wrong Ones. New York: Clarkson N. Potter, Inc., 1985. 103-109. Book.

Cowan, Connell & Kinder, Melvyn. "Chapter Nine: Freedom from Love Obsessions." Connell Cowan, Melvyn Kinder. Smart Women, Foolish Choices: Finding the RIght Men and Avoiding the Wrong Ones. New York: Clark N. Potter, Inc., 1985. 120-136. Book.

Coontz, Stephanie. "Chapter 1: The Radical Idea of Marrying for Love." Coontz, Stephanie. Marriage, a History: How Love Conquered Marriage. New York: Penguin Group (USA) Inc., 2006. 15-23. Book.

Coontz, Stephanie. "Chapter 15: Winds of Change: Marriage in the 1960s and 1970s." Coontz, Stephanie. Marriage, a History: From Obedience to Intimacy or How Love Conquered Marriage. New York: Viking Penquin, a member of Penquin Group (USA) Inc., 2005. 252. Book.

Coontz, Stephanie. "Chapter 15: Winds of Change: Marriage in the 1960s and 1970s." Coontz, Stephanie. Marriage, a History: From Obedience to Intimacy or How Love

Conquered Marriage. New York: Viking Penquin, a member of Penquin Group (USA) Inc., 2005. 250. Book.

Coontz, Stephanie. "Introduction." Coontz, Stephanie. Marriage, a History: How Love Conquered Marriage. New York: Penguin Group (USA) Inc., 2006. 1-12. Book.

Coontz, Stephanie. "Soap Operas of the Ancient World." Coontz, Stephanie. Marriage, a History: How Love Conquered Marriage. New York: Penguin Group (USA) inc., 2005. 53-69. Book.

Coontz, Stephanie. "The Many Meanings of Marriage." Coontz, Stephanie. Marriage, a History: How Love Conquered Marriage. New York: Penguin Group (USA) Inc., 2006. 24-33. Book.

Douglas, Jack. "The Ulitmate Costs of the Retreat From Marriage and Family Life." The Retreat From Marriage: Causes and Consequences. Ed. Bryce J. Christensen. Lanham: University Press of America, Inc., 1990. 55-73. Book.

Eberstadt, Nicholas. "Chapter 1: The Collapse of Work in the Second Gilded Age." Eberstadt, Nicholas. Men Without Work: America's Invisible Crisis. West Conshohocken: Templeton Press, 2016. 9-17. Book.

Eberstadt, Nicholas. "Chapter 3: Postwar America's Great Male Flight from Work." Eberstadt, Nicholas. Men Without Work: America's Invisible Crisis. New York: Templeton Press, 2016. 32-46. Book.

Eberstadt, Nicholas. "Chapter 5: Who Is He? A Statistical Portrait of the Un-Working American Man." Eberstadt, Nicholas. Men Without Work: America's Invisible Crisis. West Conshohocken: Templeton Press, 2016. 61-77. Book.

Elizabeth Barnett, Michele Casper. "A Definition of "Social Environment"." American Journal of Public Health 91.3 (2001): 465. Journal Article.

George A. Akerlof, Janet L. Yellen and Michael L. Katz. "An Analysis of Out-of-Wedlock Childbearing in the United States." The Quarterly Journal of Economics 111.2 (1996): 277-317. Journal Article. 21 August 2018. <http://www.jstor.org/stable/2946680>.

George A. Akerlof, Janet L. Yellen. "New mothers, not married: Technology shock, the demist of shotgun marriage, and the increase in out-of-wedlock births." 1 September 1996. Brookings Institute. Article. 21 August 2018. <https://www.brookings.edu/articles/new-mothers-not-married-technology-shock-the-demise-of-shotgun-marriage-and-the-increase-in-out-of-wedlock-births/>.

Glenn, Norval. "The Social and Cultural Meaning of Contemporary Marriage." The Retreat From Marriage: Causes and Consequences. Ed. Bryce J. Christensen. Lanham: University Press of America, Inc., 1990. 33-54. Book.

Goldsmith, Barton. "10 Things Your Relationship Needs to Thrive." 4 March 2013. Psychology Today. Website. 18 October 2018. <https://www.psychologytoday.com/us/blog/emotional-fitness/201303/10-things-your-relation-

ship-needs-thrive>.

Haskins, Ron and Isabel Sawhill. "Work and Marriage: The Way to End Poverty and Welfare." Welfare Reform & Beyond September 2003: 8. Policy Brief. 23 August 2018. <https://www.brookings.edu/wp-content/uploads/2016/06/pb28.pdf>.

Kathryn Edin, Maria Kefalas. "3. How Does the Dream Die?" Kathryn Edin, Maria Kefalas. Promises I Can Keep: Why Poor Women Put Motherhood Before Marriage. Berkeley, Los Angeles: University of California Press, 2005. 71-103. Book.

Kathryn Edin, Maria Kefalas. "3. How Does the Dream Die?" Kathryn Edin, Maria Kefalas. Promises I Can Keep: Why Poor Women Put Motherhood Before Marriage. Berkeley, Los Angeles: University of California Press, 2005. 71-103. Book.

Kathryn Edin, Maria Kefalas. "4. What Marriage Means." Kathryn Edin, Maria Kefalas. Promises I Can Keep: Why Poor Women Put Motherhood Before Marriage. Berkeley, Los Angeles: University California Press, 2005. 104-137. Book.

Kathryn Edin, Maria Kefalas. "Introduction." Kathryn Edin, Maria Kefalas. Promises I Can Keep: Why Poor Women Put Motherhood Before Marriage. Berkeley and Los Angeles: University of California Press, 2005. 1-26. Book.

Kenrick, Douglas T. "Evolutionary Psychology." 7 December 2018. Encyclopaedia Britannica. inc. Encyclopaedia Britannica. Website. 15 February 2019. <https://www.britannica.com/science/evolutionary-psychology>.

Merriam Webster Dictionary. domestic partner, n.2. Prod. Merriam Webster. 5 April 2019. Online. 5 April 2019. <https://www.merriam-webster.com/dictionary/domestic%20partner>.

Mundy, Liza. "Eight: Sex and the Self-Sufficient Girl." Munday, Liza. The Richer Sex: How the New Majority of Female Breadwinners Is Transforming Sex, Love, and Family. New York: Simon & Schuster, 2012. 155-174. Book.

Mundy, Liza. "Part One: The Big Flip: The New Providers." Mundy, Liza. The Richer Sex: How the New Majority of Female Breadwinners Is Tranforming Sex, Love, and Family. New York: Simon & Schuster, 2012. 3-19. Book.

Mundy, Liza. "Part One: The Overtaking." Mundy, Liza. The Richer Sex: How the new majority of femal breadwinners is transforming sex, love, and family. New York: Simon & Schuster, 2012. 38-67. Book.

OFFICE OF THE ASSISTANT SECRETARY. "United States Department of Education Office of Civil Rights." 4 April 2011. U.S. Department of Education. Document. 25 April 2019. <https://www2.ed.gov/about/offices/list/ocr/letters/colleague-201104.pdf>.

Oxford University Press. common law, n.2. Prod. OED Online. 5 April 2019. Online. 5 April 2019. <https://en.oxforddictionaries.com/definition/common_law>.

—. "Definition of business in English:." n.d. Oxford English Dictionaries. Website. 20 October 2018. <https://en.oxforddictionaries.com/definition/business>.

—. "Definition of economics in English:." n.d. Oxford English Dictionaries. Website. 20 October 2018. <https://en.oxforddictionaries.com/definition/economics>.

—. finance, n.1. Prod. OED Online. February 2019. Web. 11 February 2019.

—. hedonistic, adj. 1. Prod. OED Online. 5 April 2019. Online. 5 April 2019. <https://en.oxforddictionaries.com/definition/hedonistic>.

—. nemesis, n.1. Prod. OED Online. February 2019. Web. 11 February 2019.

—. social contract, n.1. Prod. OED Online. 11 April 2019. Online. 11 April 2019. <https://en.oxforddictionaries.com/definition/social_contract>.

—. theory, n.1. Prod. OED Online. 11 February 2019. Web. 11 February 2019. <https://en.oxforddictionaries.com/definition/theory>.

Pinker, Steven. "Chapter 1: The Official Theory." Pinker, Steven. The Blank Slate: The Modern Denial of Human

Nature. New York: Viking Penguin, a member of Penguin Putnam Inc., 2002. Book.

Quigley, Carroll. "Historical Analysis." Quigley, Carroll. The Evolution of Civilizations An Introduction to Historical Analysis. New York: Macmillan Company, 1961. 101-102. Book.

Quigley, Carroll. "Man and Culture." Quigley, Carroll. The Evolution of Civilizations: An Introduction to Historical Analysis. New York: Macmillan Company, 1961. 49-65. Book.

Reeves, Richard V. and Edward Rodrigue. "Single Black female BA seeks educated husband: Race, assortative mating and inequality." 9 April 2015. The Brookings Institution. Website. 27 August 2018. <https://www.brookings.edu/research/single-black-female-ba-seeks-educated-husband-race-assortative-mating-and-inequality/>.

Rifkin, Jeremy. "16. A New Social Contract." Rifkin, Jeremy. The End of Work: The Decline of the Global Labor Force and the Dawn of the Post-Market Era. New York: G. P. Putnam's Sons, 1995. 236-248. Book.

Rosin, Hann. "The New American Matriarchy: The Middle Class Gets A Sex Change." Rosin, Hanna. The End of Men and the Rise of Women. New York: Penguin Group (USA) Inc., 2012. 79-112. Book.

Rosin, Hanna. "Hearts of Steel: Single Girls Master the Hook Up." Rosin, Hanna. The End of Men and the Rise of

Women. New York: Penguin Group (USA) Inc., 2012. 17-46. Book.

Rosin, Hanna. "Introduction." Rosin, Hanna. The End of Men and the Rise of Women. New York: Penguin Group (USA) Inc., 2012. 1-16. Book.

Rubin, Beth A. "Marriage, Family, and a House in the Suburbs." Rubin, Beth A. Shifts in the Social Contract: Understanding Change in American Society. Thousand Oaks: Pine Forge Press, 1996. 10-13. Book.

Rubin, Beth A. "Society in Transition." Rubin, Beth A. Shifts in the Social Contract: Understanding Social Change in American Society. Thousand Oaks: Pine Forge Press, 1996. 4. Book.

Rubin, Beth A. "The American Dream." Rubin, Beth A. Shifts in the Social Contract: Understanding Change in American Society. Thousand Oaks: Pine Forge Press, 1996. 7-8. Book.

Samuel, Henry. Couples who share the housework are more likely to divorce, study finds. 27 September 2012. Website. 5 April 2019. <https://www.telegraph.co.uk/news/worldnews/europe/9572187/Couples-who-share-the-housework-are-more-likely-to-divorce-study-finds.html>.

Smith, Helen. "Chapter 1: The Marriage Strike; Why Men Don't Get Marry." Smith, Helen. Men on Strike: Why Men Are Boycotting Marriage, Fatherhood, and the American Dream - and Why It Matters. First. New York: Encounter

Books, 2013. 1-40. Book.

Smith, Helen. "Chapter 3: The College Strike: Where the Boys Aren't." Smith, Helen. Men on Strike: Why Men Are Boycotting Marriage, Fatherhood, and the American Dream-and Why it Matters. First. New York: Encounter Books, 2013. 65-94. Book.

Smith, Helen. "Chapter 5: Why it Matters." Smith, Helen. Men on Strike: Why Men Are Boycotting Marriage, Fatherhood, and the American Dream - and Why It Matters. First. New York: Encounter Books, 2013. 119-140. Book.

Smith, Herbert L. "Current Trends in Nonmarital Fertility and Divorce." The Retreat From Marriage: Causes and Consequences. Ed. Bryce J. Christensen. Lanham: University Press America, Inc., 1990. 1-31. Book.

Thomas Hansen, Britt Slagsvold. Likestilling hjemme (Equality at home). Oslo: NOVA, 2012. Report. 5 April 2019. <http://www.hioa.no/Om-OsloMet/Senter-for-velferds-og-arbeidslivsforskning/NOVA/Publikasjonar/Rapporter/2012/Likestilling-hjemme>.

Tomassi, Rollo. "BLUE PILL CONDITIONING AND EQUALISM." 17 April 2017. The Rational Male: Demystifying Intersexual Dynamics. Website. 26 August 2018. <https://therationalmale.com/2017/04/17/blue-pill-conditioning-and-equalism/>.

Tomassi, Rollo. "Defining Alpha." Tomassi, Rollo. The Rational Male. Counterflow Media, LLC, 2013. 27-29. Book.

Tomassi, Rollo. "Just Be Yourself: We are who we say we are." Tomassi, Rollo. The Rational Male. Counterflow Media, LLC, 2013. 125-127. Book.

—. "THE LIE OF EQUALITY." 22 September 2017. The Rational Male: Demystifying Intersexual Dynamics. Website. 28 August 2018. <https://therationalmale.com/2017/09/22/the-lie-of-equality/>.

—. "The Myth of the Alpha Female." 12 August 2018. The Rational Male: Demystifying Intersexual Dynamics. Website. 26 August 2018. <https://therationalmale.com/2018/08/12/the-myth-of-the-alpha-female/>.

U.S. Census Bureau, Current Population Survey, March and Annual Social and Economic Supplements. "Historical Marital Status Tables." November 2018. U. S. Census Bureau. Document. 30 April 2019. <https://www.census.gov/data/tables/time-series/demo/families/marital.html>.

Vernon A. Musselman, Eugene H. Hughes. "One: American Business and Our Economic Environment." Vernon A. Musselman, Eugene H. Hughes. Introduction to Modern Business: Analysis and Interpretation. Englewood Cliffs: Prentice-Hall, Inc., 1973. 3-33. Book.

Vitali, Agnese and Ann Berrington. "Happy families? Male acceptance of equality in the home could define the future." 12 May 2016. The Conversation. Website. 29 August 2018. <https://theconversation.com/happy-families-male-acceptance-of-equality-in-the-home-could-define-the-fu-

ture-58839>.

Wattenberg, Ben J. "Part One, What Happened and Why?: 1. The Story of This Book." Wattenberg, Ben J. Fewer: How the New Demography of Depopulation Will Shape Our Future. Chicago: Ivan R. Dee, 2004. 5-18. Book.

Whelan, Christine B. Why You Should Worry about the Widening Marriage Gap Diverging demographics may mean trouble ahead. 15 October 2010. Website. 31 August 2018. <https://www.psychologytoday.com/us/blog/life-101/201010/why-you-should-worry-about-the-widening-marriage-gap>.

Wikipedia. "Birth dearth." 27 July 2018. Wikipedia. Website. 20 October 2018. <https://en.wikipedia.org/wiki/Birth_dearth>.

—. List of regions of the United States. 30 April 2019. Website. 7 May 2019. <https://en.wikipedia.org/wiki/List_of_regions_of_the_United_States>.

—. Manosphere. 9 April 2019. Online. 10 April 2019. <https://en.wikipedia.org/wiki/Manosphere>.

World Health Organization. Total Fertility Rate. 2019. Website. 24 April 2019. <http://www.searo.who.int/entity/health_situation_trends/data/chi/TFR/en/>.

www.ingramcontent.com/pod-product-compliance
Lightning Source LLC
Chambersburg PA
CBHW052107070526
44584CB00017B/2369